AF481116

Footsteps Through Fontenelle Forest

The Omaha Walking Club, 1919-Today

Footsteps Through Fontenelle Forest

The Omaha Walking Club, 1919-Today

Marlene K. Kasza

Cover photo: Omaha Walking Club's Shack (ca. 1928)

Table of Contents

Introduction

Stepping onto the winding trails of Fontenelle Forest in 1919, a group of Omaha residents sought more than mere exercise. They craved connection—with the land, with one another, and with something greater than daily city life. From their first tentative footsteps through dense woods, they forged traditions that would outlast generations and reshape their relationship with nature.

This book invites you on every mile of that journey: through vintage papers and fading photographs, into storm-scarred clearings and sunlit understories, alongside the people whose footsteps carved over a century of trails.

Chapter 1:
Gathered to Walk, Built to Last

In the spring of 1919, Omaha was buzzing with postwar energy and a hunger for fresh-air fellowship. On a crisp March afternoon, a group of twenty-four people—teachers, clerks, businessmen, housewives, and returning veterans—gathered at the end of the Albright streetcar line for a walk to Coffin Springs in Fontenelle Forest. They shared a simple desire: to escape the city's bustle, breathe deeply in the forest, and forge new bonds outside the city. Within a short time, they planted a seed that would grow into the Omaha Walking Club.

The First Steps

That inaugural hike on March 30, 1919 stretched miles, winding along the bluffs above the Missouri River. As the group walked through the forest, something remarkable took hold. Laughter echoed beneath oak canopies. Tough veterans found solace in civilian camaraderie. Women celebrated their upcoming independence on equal footing. Edwin Jewell, recently new from Chicago and invited by co-founder Allie Houston to the first walk, later wrote about the club's founding:[1]

> …without plan and without leadership the happy group wandered through Childs Woods (now Fontenelle Forest Reserve) and stopped for rest and refreshment near Coffin Spring (Coffin Spring is located where the Camp Gifford highway crosses the Burlington Railway tracks). After members of the party were comfortably seated on stumps and fallen trees, Mr. Jewell took advantage of the opportunity to give a talk on Chicago's Prairie Club activities. A suggestion that a similar organization be formed in Omaha met with enthusiastic approval. Within ten minutes Miss Edith Tobitt had been elected President; Miss Allie Houston, Treasurer; and Mrs. George Morton, Secretary, for the balance of the year…

By the time they returned to the streetcar station, tired and exhilarated, the walking club had been unofficially founded.

Traditions are Adopted

The Omaha Walking Club was born not with a grand proclamation, but with a walk in the woods. After that inaugural walk, the name was chosen—unpretentious and practical. But a name alone does not make a fellowship. Customs were needed. And so, the early members, with a blend of earnestness and whimsy, began to adopt habits that would soon become cherished traditions.[3]

The very next day, Bulletin No. 1 was issued—a modest newsletter listing upcoming walks and club news. It was the first of many, a paper trail of footsteps and fellowship. From the beginning, "regular walks" were held on Sunday afternoons, numbered and scheduled with the precision of a train timetable each spring and fall. Other walks that were unnumbered were left to the whims of the club's members.[1]

After each walk, members gathered for coffee and "eats." The ritual was simple: bring a light lunch and a cup, toss a coin into the collection tin, and let the fire do the rest. In those early years, coffee was brewed over open flames. The club's logo—a pot suspended over a campfire—was not just a symbol, but a memory. Registered officially in 1927, it captured the essence of those smoky, joyful afternoons. As Edwin Jewell wrote, "The value of our campfire multiplies tremendously when we recall the many circles of happy faces, the amusing incidents, the songs, the hearty laughter, and the delicious odors of burning wood and boiling coffee—things that cannot be incorporated into a picture."[2]

To keep the club afloat, annual dues of fifty cents were voted for and paid to the treasurer. By the first annual meeting, held on January 9, 1920, at the South Omaha Branch Library, the dues were raised to a full dollar—a move that ensured coffee and camaraderie could continue uninterrupted. That meeting also marked the beginning of another tradition: the election of the official Board.[2]

Around this time, Edwin Jewell began work on a club handbook—a guide to walking, but also to belonging. And at the second annual meeting, the club's literary spirit took center stage with the debut of the "Hiker's Hammer." This one-copy periodical, read aloud each January, invited members to contribute prose, verse, or song—praising or playfully roasting their fellow walkers. It was the highlight of the evening, enjoyed by all, regardless of whose name was struck by its mighty blows. Though eventually discontinued, the Hammer left behind echoes of laughter and lyricism.[3]

Irma Gross (editor of the Home Economics section of the Bee newspaper and the club's first Hiker's Hammer), Hattie Mueller (charter member and 1922 president), and Frances Schwalenberg—all three were club members in 1920
Photo courtesy of Doug Wenger

These traditions—some enduring, some fleeting—formed the backbone of the Omaha Walking Club. They were not imposed, but adopted, one step at a time. And like the walks themselves, they were best enjoyed in good company, with a cup in hand and a fire crackling nearby.

Building Community

The Omaha Walking Club's story may have been sparked by a single walk, but its foundation was built on people—twenty-four of them, to be exact. On March

30, 1919, a diverse group of curious and spirited individuals gathered for what would become the club's inaugural outing. Among them were Edith Tobitt, Edwin Jewell, Mrs. Helen Morton, Allie Houston, Corrine Armstrong, Lila Bowen, Nona Bridges, Dave Broadwell, Margaret Colvin, Evelyn Dudley, Bess Dumont, Blanche Eads, Ula Echols, Juliette Griffin, Mrs. A. Grimm, Harry Grimm, Jennie Hultman, Ernest Misner, George T. Morton, Harriet Mueller, Ella Phelps, Corinne Poissant, Mrs. Isabel Robbins, and Ruth Stokes. Their shared steps marked more than the start of a club—they laid the groundwork for a community that would grow, evolve, and welcome thousands more into its fold.[2]

What followed was nothing short of a groundswell. By late May, the club had grown to 87 members.[4] By August, 136.[5] And by December, 175.[6] The trails weren't just being walked—they were being woven into the social fabric of the club's members.

In its first year alone, the club scheduled 29 official walks, covering 185 miles. The average turnout was 34 walkers per outing—a testament to the club's magnetic pull. These weren't just strolls through nature; they were shared experiences, each step strengthening the bonds between members.[2]

By 1920, the club had evolved beyond its original purpose. It was no longer simply a gathering of nature enthusiasts—it was a community. Trust, ritual, and a love for open trails became its foundation. Weekend walks were joined by swim parties every Monday evening at Sandy Point, a beach at Carter Lake, where laughter echoed off the water and friendships deepened under the summer sky.[1]

The momentum didn't stop. By 1922, the club's membership roll peaked at 378—a number that reflected not just popularity, but belonging. The club had become a place where strangers became companions, and companions became lifelong friends.[1]

Evolution of the Club

From its earliest days, the Omaha Walking Club was more than a group of weekend wanderers—it was a living, breathing organism, constantly adapting to the needs, quirks, and ambitions of its members.

The first annual meeting in January 1920, held at the South Omaha Public Library, set the tone for what would become a cherished tradition. Officers were elected—Edwin Jewell as president, George Morton as vice-president, Hattie Mueller as secretary, and Allie Houston as treasurer. Morton's lantern slides of "picturesque Omaha" lit up the room, and prizes were awarded for the best "Kodak" snapshots taken during the year. The club was already blending governance with celebration, and the results were delightfully democratic.[7]

But evolution wasn't limited to leadership—it extended to wardrobe. In the club's first walks, members dressed as if headed to a garden party rather than a dirt trail. Women quickly discovered that long dresses and rugged terrain were a poor match. In 1938, longtime member and South High teacher Irene Tauchen recalled the clever workaround in the early years: women wore skirts over their knickers to ride the streetcar, then shed the skirts at the trailhead. She remembered one walk where her skirt went missing, leaving her to ride home in knickers—mortified, but undeterred.[8]

Dr. Harold Gifford Sr. leading the Omaha Walking Club through Fontenelle Forest Reserve on April 20, 1919

The second annual meeting was held in January 1921. The new officers were elected—Allie Houston as president, Edith Tobitt as first vice-president, Edwin Jewell as second vice-president, Irene Higbee as treasurer, and Hattie Mueller as secretary. A constitution and by-laws were adopted.[9]

The club's voice grew louder with the introduction of the "Hiker's Hammer," a paper edited by Irma Gross and distributed at this meeting. One of its earliest entries, "Public Opinion" by Lyman T. Williams, captured the bemused reactions of onlookers as the club's "rabble" marched past. The club, it seemed, was already delighting in its own eccentricity.[9]

PUBLIC OPINION

South of Bellevue or north of Florence
Our straggling cohorts the villagers view.
With mild disdain or with deep abhorrence
They stand and gaze and they gaze anew;
And when the last of our sweatered rabble
Has passed from the range of their staring eyes,
With one consent they begin to gabble
And mock and murmur and criticize.

Surely they come from the State Asylum;
Surely their brains are none of the best:
Or what mad fancy could thus beguile 'em
To work so hard on their day of rest?
It matters not if the sun shines hotly
Or the bleak rain washes the roads to mire;
It's all the same to these folks in motley
If they shake with cold or with heat perspire ...

--LYMAN T. WILLIAMS

In November 1920, Dr. Harold Gifford gifted the club a three-room house near Wiley Point. Dubbed "the Shack," it became a hub for gatherings, games, and coffee-fueled camaraderie. Though this original shack later burned, the club maintained a clubhouse in or near Fontenelle Forest for nearly a century. Members pitched in money for remodeling the Shack and adopted a constitution and by-laws to guide their growing community.[2]

The Shack ran on elbow grease and egalitarian spirit. Doctors split wood, stenographers swept floors, and bank executives rolled the tennis court. Sunday hosts were assigned to light lamps, sweep rooms, collect dues, and ensure the coffee water was hot. Rules were posted: register upon arrival, pay a

The "Shack" * 1921

small activity fee, and absolutely no firearms. Cars were to be parked at the "Donut House," a cabin by the forest entrance where donuts were sold—and the 2-1/2 mile Walking Club trail was to be used to reach the Shack.[2]

By 1921, the club had formalized its structure with committees for Membership, Walks, Camp, Vacation Outings, Photographs and Slides, and Conservation. These committees didn't just plan—they shaped the club's identity. Walks multiplied, with two or three scheduled each weekend. Annual trips to mountains and lakes became tradition.[2]

By 1922, weekend parties included overnight stays in gender-separated tents, with overflow campers bedding down on grassy riverbanks. Quiet hours were strictly observed from 11:30 p.m. to 6:00 a.m.—a nod to both civility and exhaustion.[10]

Annual dues evolved with the times: 50 cents at the start, raised to $1.00 in 1920, then $3.00 in 1951, $5.00 in 1976, and eventually $15.00 today. A small fee for walks and activities was once charged but has since been dropped, keeping the club accessible and welcoming.[2]

In March 1929, the club celebrated its tenth anniversary with 250 members. In that first decade, there were 415 Sunday walks, 28,000 sign-ins at the Shack, and more than 100 members had married within the club—a testament to the power of shared trails and the enjoyment of each other's company.[11] Tennis, volleyball, swimming in the river, and horseshoes were popular at the Shack, turning it into a year-round playground.[3]

The Great Depression brought a dip in membership—150 by 1934,[12] and just 119 by 1938.[13] But the spirit endured. In 1937, the board introduced "Homecoming Day" for current and former members, a tradition that would last for decades. The silver anniversary in 1944 was marked by a silver-covered program booklet celebrating "husbands and wives, congenial comrades, lasting friends, health, a new freedom and the real joy of living."[2]

That December, the annual meeting was held at the Castle Hotel. Eighty members and guests attended, including six who had been there from the beginning. Letters from club members serving in the armed forces were read aloud, bridging the distance between battlefield and forest trail.[14]

After the war, membership rebounded to 142 in 1946,[15] though it dipped again to 108 by 1953.[1] Through it all, the Omaha Walking Club remained a resilient, evolving community—one that could weather economic hardship, war, and wardrobe malfunctions with equal grace.

The Shack, that beloved hub of muddy boots and boiling coffee, stood firm through weather in the early decades—except once. On Sunday, March 20, 1960, a 27-inch blanket of snow smothered the trails, with drifts so deep they swallowed footsteps whole. For the first and only time in club history, the Official Board closed the Shack doors. But tradition is a stubborn thing. The scheduled hostess and three venturesome friends, undeterred, battled the drifts to reach the Shack, taking twice the usual time. Joe Burke, the lone man in the group, was nearly lost in the snowbanks. The Heno Hike was cancelled, as was the River Hike north of Florence the following week. Yet on March 27, the hike leader and a few sturdy souls pressed on, determined to walk the scouted trail. Snow or no snow, the club's heartbeat never missed a beat.[2]

"Most popular place after the hike is the shack, above." Homecoming in April 1940
Omaha World-Herald

In 1969, the club celebrated its golden milestone. The 50th anniversary was a jubilant affair, with a full slate of activities. Ken Wenger and early-day member Bill Coons led a commemorative walk through Fontenelle Forest, retracing the steps of the original 1919 hike. Co-founder Allie Houston joined Mr. and Mrs. Charley Gadway—one of the first couples to marry within the club—at the Nature Center to share stories and preview the festivities. Events included a photo show at Commercial Savings and Loan on April 19, a homecoming banquet at the New Tower Motor Inn on May 17, an open house at the Shack on May 18, and an expedition to the Grand Tetons from July 4–13. Special walks continued into the fall, each one a tribute to the club's enduring legacy.[16]

By 1971, the club boasted around 200 members, ranging in age from 16 to 90.[17] The trails were alive with voices spanning generations and stories passed from one walker to the next. By 1979, the club's 60th year, membership had grown to 235, with a noticeable uptick in younger hikers joining the ranks.[18] The club was evolving again—back into a multigenerational community, where seasoned walkers passed down trail wisdom to newcomers with fresh legs and eager hearts.

Homecoming Day in the 1980s and 1990s remained a highlight of the calendar, transformed into themed celebrations that blended nostalgia with playful creativity. Members dressed up for "Hobo Athletes," "Mexican Fiesta," "Style Show," "U.S.A.," "Pioneers," "Indians," and "School Reunion." The Shack became a stage for laughter, costumes, and storytelling—a place where history was not just remembered but relived.[1]

By 2001, membership had dipped to 118. The original clubhouse site with sleeping quarters had been lost nine years prior and was felt deeply. Then came the flood of 2019, which destroyed the clubhouse they were using at that time, followed by the global pandemic in 2020–2021. These years tested the club's resilience, but the spirit remained intact.[1]

On July 19, 2019, the club marked its Centennial Celebration on a sweltering 100-degree day at the Fontenelle Nature Center. Fifty members and guests gathered, including representatives from Fontenelle Forest and the Sarpy County Museum. Longtime member Doug Wenger returned from Monterey, California to speak about the club's early history. He shared slides of past adventures, many featuring his parents, who had joined in the 1930s. The day was hot, but the stories? Full of heart, history, and the kind of kinship you don't forget.[1]

Through snowstorms and celebrations, dips and revivals, the Omaha Walking Club has never stopped walking. Its evolution is not just a tale of numbers and events—it's a story of people who kept showing up, year after year, trail after trail, to build something lasting. A community. A tradition. A legacy on foot.

Chapter 2:
Fontenelle Forest: A Natural Sanctuary

For over a century, the Omaha Walking Club and Fontenelle Forest grew side by side—two institutions rooted in a shared love of nature. Founded in the same decade, their histories are intertwined.

The club maintained a clubhouse on or near forest land for nearly 100 years. Reaching it was part of the ritual: members walked through the woods to arrive, turning each visit into a journey. With its winding trails, towering oaks, and hushed ravines, the forest wasn't just scenery—it was sanctuary.

Fontenelle Forest long stood as more than a backdrop to the walking club—it was a living companion, a quiet witness to decades of footsteps, laughter, and reflection. From early club outings to solitary wanderings, the forest became a place where members found challenge, camaraderie, and a deeper sense of belonging.

Layers of Time in the Trees

Long before Fontenelle Forest became a sanctuary for hikers and naturalists, its hills and hollows bore witness to centuries of change. The land was once open grassland, dotted with bur oaks and shaped by fire and grazing. By the early 1900s, much of the forest had been logged to support the area's growing infrastructure, and parts were later used as a dairy farm. As a result of this logging, most trees are less than a century old in some areas of the forest—yet the forest still whispers its past.[19]

Clues along the southern trails of the forest led historians to uncover the site of the Lucien Fontenelle Trading Post, a vital stop during the Rocky Mountain fur trade and later an Indian Agency. This post helped establish Bellevue, Nebraska's oldest community. Nearby, a marker commemorates the burial site of Logan Fontenelle, the forest's namesake. Logan was the son of Lucien Fontenelle and his mother was the daughter of Chief Big Elk of the Omaha tribe. Half French, half Indian, Logan served as an interpreter between the government and the Indians. He was tragically killed and scalped by Sioux warriors in 1855 while on a hunting trip. Though his exact burial site remains unknown, a gravestone placed in the forest decades later honors his legacy.[20]

Fontenelle Forest is historical ground. Its upland ridges hold shallow depressions—remnants of prehistoric dwellings—and the remains of Indian earth lodges. Archaeological evidence reveals that diverse Indigenous cultures once flourished here. A nearby trail points to Logan Fontenelle's grave and another marker notes the 1846 Mormon encampment, giving Mormon Hollow its name. The forest itself is also part of the Lewis and Clark National Historic Trail.[19]

The small settlement of Wiley, named for a man who once operated a ferry across the river,[21] once stood at the current site of Hidden Lake. Over time, the river reclaimed it—leaving no trace behind.[22]

The land saw many changes after the Trading Post: a channelized river, railroads, roads, and even an Army practice range near the southwest end of History Trail from 1887 to 1895.[19]

In the early 1900's, Dr. Robert Gilder, an archaeologist and artist, lived at "Wake Robin," his log cabin and studio in a wooded lot near the forest's edge. His paintings captured the forest's quiet beauty, and his archaeological studies helped preserve its deeper story. Dr. Gilder's property, on Grove Road, was eventually sold and repurposed in the 1960's to be used for youth groups.[19]

*Dr. Robert Gilder at his Wake Robin cabin * photo courtesy of Fontenelle Forest*

In the spring of 1919, as the Omaha Walking Club took its first steps, construction was underway at Wiley Point for Camp Gifford—soon to become the largest Boy Scout camp in the nation.[23] Plans were in motion to open a sprawling swimming pool by August of that year, and in its heyday, the camp welcomed hundreds of scouts each summer. But the site's lowland location proved vulnerable. After years of repeated flooding, Camp Gifford was closed in the early

1940s. In 1947, it was succeeded by Camp Wa-Kon-Da,[24] built on higher ground to carry forward the scouting tradition.[21]

Today, the forest stands not only as a haven for wildlife and walkers, but as a living archive—where every trail bends through history, and every rustling leaf carries the memory of those who walked here long before.

From Bluff to Preserve: Fontenelle Forest's Founding

The idea for Fontenelle Forest began not with trees, but around a table. In 1910, Bellevue College professor Dr. Ansel A. Tylor gathered with friends at the home of Mr. and Mrs. Lowrie Childs to share a bold vision: to preserve the woodlands along the Missouri River between Omaha and Bellevue. Though initial efforts to establish a state park fell short, the group persisted. In 1913, they formed a private, non-profit nature association with a self-perpetuating Board of Trustees and elected officers. The Fontenelle Forest Association was born.[19]

By 1916, the association began seriously considering land acquisition, but World War I made fundraising difficult. That's when Dr. Harold Gifford Sr., a respected Omaha physician and conservationist, stepped in. He purchased the tract of land on Child's Point—a wooded bluff overlooking the river—to hold until the association could buy it outright. Fundraising gained momentum by 1919, and in 1920, the association purchased 367 acres from Dr. and Mrs. Gifford for $49,500, with the Giffords donating an additional $7,500 toward the sale.[19]

Dr. A. A. Tyler * photo courtesy of Fontenelle Forest

The signing of the land purchase was a landmark moment, attended by several notable figures including Roy N. Towl, a civil engineer and one of the association's original founders. This first tract of Fontenelle Forest, located on Child's Point, laid the foundation for decades of conservation and community engagement.[19] Just east of it lay Wiley Point, another area of the forest that would later host Camp Gifford and the Omaha Walking Club's earliest hikes.[23]

Generosity continued to shape the forest's growth. In 1925, Mrs. Sarah Joslyn donated 100 acres, followed by 175 acres gifted by Dr. Gifford and his heirs in 1925 and 1931. In 1940, Walking Club member George T. Morton added 10 acres to the forest's holdings. Over the years, additional acquisitions, trades, and legacies expanded the forest's footprint.[22]

*"Lowrie Childs / Child's Point" 1909 * From the KMTV/Bostwick-Frohardt Photo Collection, permanently housed at The Durham Museum*

For decades, Fontenelle Forest was a quiet refuge for hikers and picnickers, maintained by a single caretaker and volunteers. But in the 1960s, Omaha's city forester Jim Malkowski saw its potential as an educational resource. He began leading nature hikes that quickly gained popularity, and in 1966, the forest opened its first Nature Center, with Malkowski as its director. That original center was replaced in 2000 by the current facility, which continues to serve as a hub for ecological education and community connection.[19]

Today, Fontenelle Forest spans approximately 1,500 acres, a living legacy of vision, persistence, and generosity. From its earliest days on Child's Point to its role as a beloved nature preserve, the forest remains a place where history, habitat, and human curiosity meet beneath the canopy.[19]

Cottonwoods, Ravines, and Quiet Majesty

Fontenelle Forest has long offered healing, solitude, and inspiration—a quiet refuge where generations have come to walk, reflect, and reconnect with nature. Its dramatic landscape rises in steep loess ridges, sheltering a rich mix of broadleaf trees like bur oak, hickory, cottonwood, and walnut. Springs at the base of these ridges feed slow-moving streams that nourish one of the region's last spring-fed marshes. The contrast between rugged uplands and wide floodplain creates a striking and varied terrain.

Wildlife flourishes throughout the forest. Over 200 bird species have been recorded, alongside deer, beavers, mink, foxes, reptiles and amphibians. Wildflowers carpet the forest floor, and marshes draw migrating ducks and shorebirds. As a protected game reserve, Fontenelle Forest remains a place where nature thrives undisturbed.[19]

Visitors enter from Bellevue Boulevard, about a mile south of Omaha's city limits. From there, the

"Child's Point - Bellevue, Nebraska" 1919-08-16
From the KMTV/Bostwick-Frohardt Photo Collection,
permanently housed at The Durham Museum

forest stretches southeast for nearly three miles along the Missouri River. There are no roads within the forest, save for one public route leading to a floodplain parking lot. Seventeen miles of marked trails wind through upland ridges and lowland wetlands, offering quiet immersion in a landscape shaped by time and resilience.[19]

But Fontenelle Forest is not static. It is a living system, constantly evolving—and sometimes recovering. In the 1930s, the U.S. Army Corps of Engineers channelized the Missouri River, straightening its course to improve navigation.[19]

*Wing Dams in the Missouri – 1936 * OWC photo by William Coons*

In recent decades, the forest launched an ambitious experiment to recreate the oak savanna—a blend of prairie grasses and widely spaced bur oaks that once dominated the region. Restoration is complex. Without historical disturbances like fire, elk, and bison, invasive woody plants have crowded out young oaks, depriving them of sunlight.[19]

Fontenelle Forest has also weathered nature's fury. Floods have shaped its story, with major events recorded in 1881, 1943, 1952, 1967, 1978, 1993, 2011, and 2019. Ice jams, snowmelt, and intense rainfall continue to test the resilience of the land and those who care for it.[25]

But the forest remains a timeless retreat—a place where nature welcomes hikers, artists, and curious minds alike. It's not just preserved; it's alive, evolving with care and intention, offering peace and wonder with every step beneath its canopy.

The Route to the Clubhouse

In the years following the establishment of Fontenelle Forest, the number of hiking trails expanded. The July 1928 edition of Omaha Magazine published directions for reaching the club's cabin located on the forest's east side. These instructions were provided by Agnes D. Winkelman, wife of the president of the Omaha Walking Club.

To reach the camp, take the Fort Crook Interurban at Twenty-fourth and N streets to the Country Club station, climb Camp Brewster hill, and walk south to the "Donut House," the little brown house two doors south of Camp Brewster; or autos may be parked at the "Donut House." Entrance is made to the beautiful Fontenelle Reserve by way of the turnstile, pausing a moment in gratitude to those far-sighted ones of our community, who, under the inspiration of Dr. and Mrs. Gifford and of Mrs. Joslyn, secured to the public for all time this wonderful tract of bluff and bottom land. It comprises some six hundred acres reaching almost from the south line of Omaha to Bellevue.

*"Trail to the Shack" 1927 * OWC photo by Lillie Jean Busch*

Once inside the turnstile there are several routes from which to choose. The shortest, about four miles for the round trip, leads past the bird fountain erected by the Audubon Society in honor of Dr. Towne. The grassy depression so noticeable here is the site of one of Dr. Gilder's excavations, it being one of the many remains upon the hilltops of this region of the earth lodges or homes either of the Omaha tribe of Indians or some prehistoric people. In the annals of the Walking Club this is "The Bowl," a favorite place to rest and sing upon the return trip, whether the tramp is 'neath a smiling moon or a drizzling rain.

The trail leads down a gentle slope from "The Bowl" with ever changing but ever beautiful outlook of densely wooded hillside and distant river. Pause a moment at this beauty point just before the trail drops suddenly and steeply to river level. At the left is a natural amphitheater, its sides a solid mass of green in almost impenetrable thickness; at the right, hills and vales which are a billowing sea of native timber, the refuge of our rarest and most beautiful birds; the habitat of more species of birds than any other single location in the United States.

At the foot of the hill there is again a choice of trails. The shorter one follows the river; the other, beautiful Fern Trail, leads through the glen whose slopes are a solid carpet of ferns and sweet williams, with violets, dutchmen's breeches, the waxy bloodroot, Solomon's seal, the rare moccasin flower, jack-in-the-pulpit, anemone, and the lovely array of autumn flowers, each following in its turn.

New Boots, Same Trails

Though the names and faces may change, the forest remains—a quiet constant beneath shifting skies and generations of footsteps. New hikers arrive with fresh boots and curious eyes, tracing the same winding paths once walked by those who came before. Fontenelle Forest continues to offer more than scenery; it offers belonging and reflection. In these woods, history is never far behind—and the future is always just ahead, waiting at the next bend in the trail.

*"Approaching the Bowl—Fontenelle Forest" 1928 * OWC photo by Wm. A. Coons*

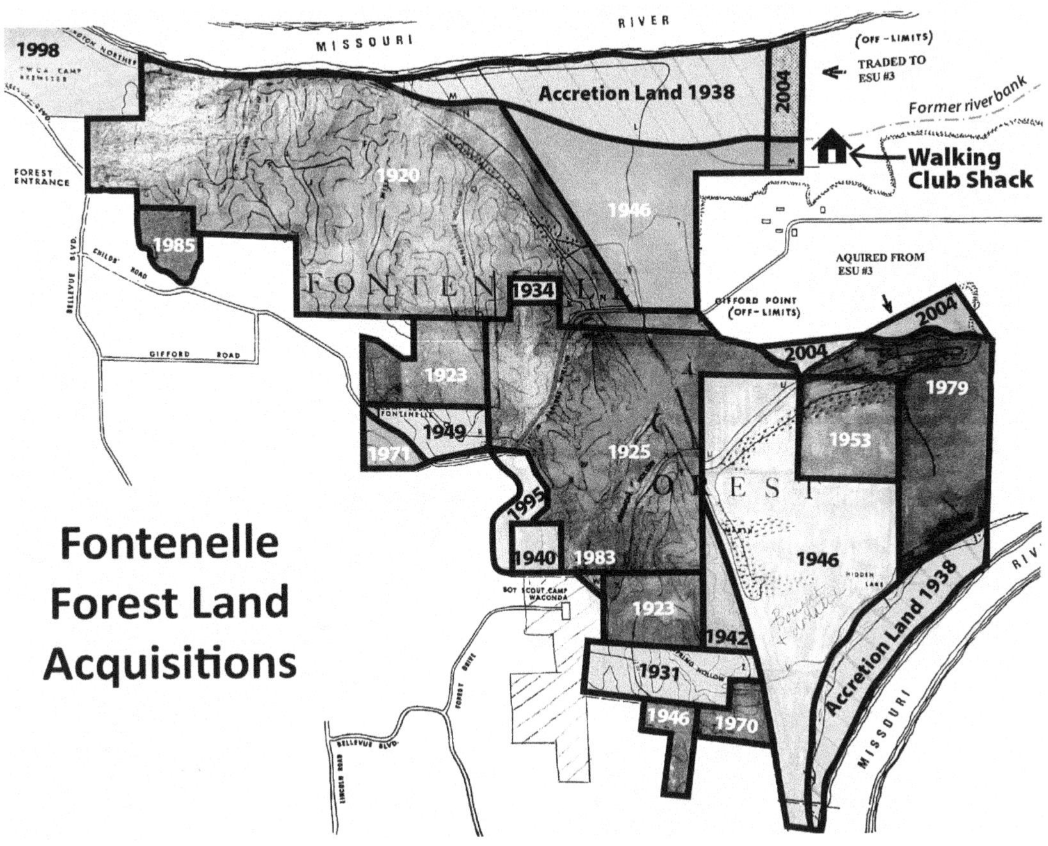

This map of Fontenelle Forest illustrates land acquisitions over time. The areas adjacent to the Missouri River, labeled "accretion land 1938," were added after river channelization, as regions previously part of the river accumulated silt and became forest land. Following these changes, the walking club's grounds ceased to border the river.

Additionally, a section west of the club's grounds was transferred to Gifford Farms (now ESU #3) through a land exchange, resulting in the former walking club grounds no longer bordering the forest as of 2004.

Chapter 3:
Sheltered in the Forest – The Clubhouses

The Omaha Walking Club has had five clubhouses throughout its history. The first three were on eight acres of leased land on Gifford property bordering Fontenelle Forest. To access this site, the club's members were required to access the trails from the parking lot on Bellevue Boulevard and hike 2-1/2 miles through the forest. These first three clubhouses were referred to as the "Shack." The final two clubhouses were at different locations—one near and one in Fontenelle Forest.

A Generous Beginning – The First Clubhouse (1921)

The club's first true home arrived not by committee or construction—but by generosity. In November 1920, Dr. Harold Gifford Sr., a respected physician and passionate advocate for nature, donated a modest three-room cabin to the club. It

*Shack #1 * photo courtesy of Doug Wenger*

stood abandoned in a field between the Boy Scout Camp and old farm buildings, waiting to be repurposed. Edward M. Kennedy spotted its potential and persuaded Dr. Gifford to allow the club to transform it into a shelter and meeting place.[2]

Jim Baldwin, Ed Kennedy, and other dedicated members rolled up their sleeves. They cleaned, repaired, tore down a partition to open the space, built benches, and gave the cabin a fresh coat of paint. In early 1921, the refurbished structure was moved to Wiley's Point—just east of the Boy Scout Camp and bordering Fontenelle Forest. Though not technically within the forest, it was reached by a 2½-mile walk through its winding trails, making the journey part of the ritual.[26]

Originally named the "Wiley Point Camp and Club House," it quickly earned a more affectionate title: "the Shack." It was simple but spirited, equipped with facilities for coffee and cooking, and governed by a straightforward rule—each member brought their own food, cooked their own meals, and cleaned up after themselves. The Shack became the heartbeat of club life: a place to gather, sing, share stories, and take shelter from Nebraska's unpredictable skies.[26]

But the joy was short-lived. On May 24, 1921—just six months later—the Shack was lost to fire. A watchman at the nearby Boy Scout Camp spotted flames and telephoned Ed Kennedy with grim urgency: "There will be nothing but cinders left in a few more minutes." The blaze consumed everything.[27]

Though the Shack was gone, its spirit endured. It marked the beginning of the club's tradition of building spaces not just for shelter, but for belonging. And thanks to Dr. Gifford's generosity, the club continued to occupy his land—laying the foundation for a future clubhouse and future hikes.[2]

Members of the Omaha Walking Club at their first shack - early 1921

STANDING ABOVE: N. J. Weston, BACK ROW: Homer F. Pennock, George T. Morton, Mrs. Morton, Maude Watson, Arthur Lyon, MIDDLE ROW: Harriet Mueller, James Baldwin, J. E. Layten, BOTTOM ROW: Judge Charles E. Foster, Charles Gadway, R. B. Miller

Rising from the Ashes – Clubhouse #2 (1921-1950)

The fire that destroyed the club's first shack in May 1921 did more than reduce a beloved gathering place to cinders—it ignited a surge of determination. By August, the Omaha Walking Club voted to adopt a new permanent camp site in the wooded area north of the original location. Dr. Harold Gifford, recognizing the fire was not due to carelessness, graciously consented to the construction of a new clubhouse on his land.[2]

At the time of the fire, the men's sleeping tent was still under construction. Jim Baldwin, ever resourceful, moved the unfinished structure to the new site, where it served as a temporary clubhouse through the summer. But members wanted more than a stopgap—they wanted a true home. At the next monthly meeting, a subscription blank was placed on a table to test the club's enthusiasm. Within minutes, pledges exceeded $300.[2]

Momentum built quickly. Plans were drawn, materials purchased, carpenters hired, and the sound of sawing and hammering filled the woods. To raise additional funds, Homer Pennock was authorized to host one of his famous chicken dinners, and coupon books were sold to cover costs. Excitement grew with each nail driven.[2]

The new shack was a single-room frame building, roughly 20 by 28 feet, with a large round fireplace at its center. It could accommodate 40 people around the hearth, and just as many in a second circle.[28]

*Shack #2 before the extension * photo courtesy of Doug Wenger*

On October 16, 1921, the new shack was dedicated. That afternoon, 150 people joined a record-setting hike to the site. Club president Allie Houston served steaming bowls of Mulligan stew, a dish that would later become a Depression-era staple. As dusk fell, a cornerstone ceremony unfolded with theatrical flair: N. J. Weston played the king, Nell Baldwin and Emma Kment danced, and Herman Reinholtz played a devil. A campfire followed, and for an hour, voices rose in song beneath the stars. The return home was made by moonlight, back to the Albright streetcar line.[29]

As the club grew, so did its facilities. In 1923, Mrs. Mabel B. Buchanan designed a scale model of a new wing to serve as a dining room and kitchen. Her plans were unanimously approved, and by fall, the addition was complete and paid for. Cooking and eating at the Shack became a fine art.[2]

By 1925, the clubhouse was overflowing with cots, tools, and supplies. Mr. C. F. Drake offered to build a storage shed if the club provided materials. The result was the "doghouse," a 10-by-12-foot building that housed everything from shovels and ladders to mattresses and paint. Alongside the Shack, there were sleeping tents for men and women, and the grounds eventually featured tennis, croquet, horseshoe, volleyball, and table tennis.[15] Even the outhouses had names: Petunia and Violet.[2]

*"The Shack" 1925 * OWC photo by T. B. Murray*

The club's lease agreements with the Gifford family reflected a deep respect for the land. In 1926, Dr. and Mrs. Harold Gifford Sr. granted a 25-year lease on 8⅓ acres for a nominal fee. A new lease in 1948 with Dr. Harold Gifford, Jr. included a covenant to protect the forest's flora and fauna, prohibit intoxicants and firearms, and preserve the land's natural beauty.[2]

Unfortunately, the Missouri River was a restless neighbor. In 1927, the Shack grounds flooded two feet deep. In 1943, the river rose higher than it had since 1881, washing out piers and leaving the front steps suspended in mid-air. Homecoming was postponed,[30] but the club rallied with a clean-up day. In 1944, the river returned, though less aggressively, and members navigated the soggy terrain with boots and good humor.[2]

Then came the final blow. On December 31, 1950, fire struck again. The Shack and all its contents—including irreplaceable photos and memorabilia—were lost. This had been home for the Walking Club for 29 years. The next morning, thirty members arrived to find a dreary scene. But true to form, coffee and cookies were served, dues were collected, and the first dollar was donated toward rebuilding. Shack or no shack, the club's spirit endured.

Concrete Resolve – Clubhouse for 41 years (1951-1992)

The loss of the second Shack on New Year's Eve 1950 could have marked the end of an era. Instead, it became the beginning of one. Just eleven days later, fifty-nine determined members gathered at the YWCA to plan a new clubhouse. A Building Committee and a Finance Committee were elected, and by mid-February, the club had agreed: the new shack would honor the spirit of the old but be built to last—this time with concrete blocks and a cement floor.[2]

Building shack #3 in 1951
photo courtesy of Doug Wenger

Construction began in May 1951 with members digging trenches and pouring footings. Rain delayed progress, but by July, contractor Martin Peniston was erecting walls. The roof and painting were handled by club volunteers, and by early autumn, the Shack had windows, doors, a back porch, and a new stove—generously donated by Dr. and Mrs. Harold Gifford Jr. The fireplace, a beloved centerpiece, was rebuilt exactly over the site of the original. On September 16, 1951, eighty-three members and guests gathered for Homecoming and Shack Shower Day, bringing useful gifts and renewed spirit. At the annual meeting, Charley Gadway, chairman of the Building Committee, received a rising vote of thanks. The Finance Committee reported a Shack fund of $2,623.38—built from member donations, insurance, and goodwill. The final touch was the installation of electricity in the winter of 1952.[2]

This Shack, like the previous one, had no heater but the large fire pit provided warmth in the winter. The Camp Committee in those days had the responsibility every Sunday of getting a volunteer host or hostess to start a fire during the winter to warm the building before walkers arrive. Summer could be hot inside, but there were no fans. The members just opened the windows to let any breeze flow through.[31]

The sleeping cabins were elevated on concrete blocks, screened in above waist height—breezy in summer, but drafty in storms. Hardy souls sometimes slept inside the Shack during winter, warming themselves by the large central fire pit.[13]

It was a happy club again—but not for long. Homecoming 1952 was set for May 5th, a celebration of renewal in the newly built Shack. Spirits were high, plans were made, and the camp was ready to welcome members. But on April 18, just two weeks before the festivities, Old Man River returned with a vengeance. The Missouri crested at a staggering 31.08 feet, transforming the landscape into a raging torrent from bluff to bluff. It was another major calamity for the Omaha Walking Club.[2]

Shack #3 – Built 1951

As the river began to swell and threaten the grounds, four quick-thinking members raced to the Shack that evening. With urgency, they hauled mattresses, paint, and tools inside, stacking them on tables. By sheer luck or instinct, they placed the supplies just six inches above the eventual flood line. Then came the waiting. For two long weeks, members watched the waters rise, worried, and wondered what would be left.[2]

After one failed attempt to reach the Shack, a determined crew—Ken Wenger, Harold Hatch, Charley Gadway, and Joe and Mike Burke—waded through thick mud and standing water on a Saturday morning. What greeted them was surreal: the Shack stood like an island, nearly encircled by a horseshoe-shaped lake. Ditches carved by the flood crisscrossed the grounds and trails. Inside, three inches of mud coated the floor, and a high-water mark of twenty-three inches stained the walls. One corner of the Shack's footing had been completely undermined. Every wooden building—sleeping cabins, outhouses, storage sheds—had been lifted off its foundation.[2]

With a shortage of funds after building the Shack the year before, the club faced this additional test of its spirit. Tools were borrowed, then weekend after weekend, members showed up—not for hikes, but for hard labor. They shoveled mud, hauled debris, reset buildings, and patched the wounded camp back together. The Shack's damaged corner was reinforced with cement blocks and creosoted ties. The interior was scrubbed and repainted. By fall, the ditches were filled, and the exterior refreshed.[2]

The flood had one good result. It unearthed 400 feet of unused water line, which was repurposed to pipe spring water to the Shack. Charley Gadway prepared the pipe and oversaw its installation. Over the years, modern touches were added: gas tanks and light fixtures in 1960, a sink in 1966, a new stove in 1973, and two outdoor fireplaces in 1978.[2]

The Shack's lease was renewed in 1951 with Dr. Harold Gifford Jr., and again in 1969 with The Gifford Foundation Inc., covering the grounds through the year 2000. Each lease carried a solemn covenant: to protect the land, preserve its natural beauty, and prohibit intoxicants, firearms, and fireworks. The club honored these terms with care.[1]

Through fire and flood, the Shack endured. Members parked at the Donut House and walked in, abiding by Fontenelle Forest's rule to exit by 9:00 p.m. The Shack was modernized but never lost its rustic charm. Violet and Petunia remained in service, as did the sleeping cabins, the doghouse, and a newly added woodshed. Working together, the club kept the buildings in good repair and the spirit alive.[2]

Eventually, the ownership of Gifford Farm—along with the clubhouse grounds—was donated to the State of Nebraska for educational purposes. The state became the club's new landlord. Then the property was transferred to Educational Service Unit #3 (ESU #3), a public agency that provides specialized services to area school districts, in 1989.[32]

To the shock and dismay of the walking club, it was discovered the lease to the clubhouse grounds could legally be broken if the property ever changed hands.[1] In 1992 ESU #3 made the decision to terminate the lease. The club's buildings were purchased, and after 71 years on the property, the Shack and outbuildings—built with concrete, sweat, and community—were no longer the property of the club. This was a severe blow to many members who had met their spouses there and seen their children and grandchildren grow up on that property. Shack #3 remained in use until September 1992.[33] It was the longest-serving clubhouse in the club's history, a testament to resilience and resourcefulness. The clubhouse building survived more floods through the decades and is currently used for children's programs.

On High Ground - Clubhouse #4 – (1993-2014)

After the loss of the third shack in 1992, the club faced a familiar crossroads: rebuild, relocate, or relinquish their forest gathering place. They chose resilience. Unwilling to give up the tradition of meeting near Fontenelle Forest, members turned their attention to Camp Brewster—a once-vibrant property owned by the YWCA, just north of the Nature Center and a short walk from Bellevue Boulevard.[1]

Clubhouse #4

Between 1992 and 1993, club members renovated and remodeled two dilapidated buildings on the site. One was transformed into a spacious meeting room; the other, a former bathhouse, was converted into two storage rooms and two restrooms—complete with modern plumbing and a propane heater. No more outhouses, no more floodplain. This was the first and only clubhouse safely perched above the reach of the Missouri River and a short walk from a parking lot.[1]

The new facility, referred to as the "clubhouse" rather than the "Shack," marked a shift in tone and comfort. It had electricity, ceiling fans, screened windows and doors, carpeting, and a wood-burning stove for chilly mornings. The club paid for liability insurance and maintained the buildings and grounds, having invested a total of $11,083 for the rebuild. Final approval from the City of Bellevue Building Department came on July 7, 1993.[1]

By August, the clubhouse was fully in use. Photo albums lined the shelves, and a volleyball court welcomed friendly competition. A Grand Opening was held in October, celebrating not just a new building, but the club's enduring spirit of adaptation.[1]

Camp Brewster itself carried a rich legacy. From 1905 to 1917, it had been home to the South Omaha Country Club, with tennis courts, golf links, and hiking trails. In 1917, the YWCA purchased the land and operated it as a summer camp for young women for the next 80 years. At its peak, Camp Brewster featured 23 cabins, a swimming pool with a fountain, horseback riding, archery, crafts, and more. In the late 1990s, Fontenelle Forest acquired the property, becoming the club's new landlord. That arrangement was held until 2014, when the cabin was repurposed for educational programs and public events.[19]

Though Clubhouse #4 was never truly theirs, it was warm, welcoming, and filled with the same laughter, stories, and camaraderie that had defined every clubhouse before it. It stood as a testament to the club's ability to adapt, to honor the past while embracing the present—and to find joy wherever the trail led.

The Clubhouse That Nature Reclaimed (2015-2019)

By 2015, the club had weathered decades of change, but its spirit remained unshaken. When the club found itself once again without a permanent home, it pivoted with characteristic grace—this time to the Gilbert and Martha Hitchcock Wetlands Learning Center, a modest building nestled in the forest lowlands about two miles from Fontenelle Forest's Nature Center. Typically reserved for nature classes, the center became Clubhouse #5 thanks to a generous arrangement with Fontenelle Forest: the club could use the building rent-free on Sunday afternoons, as long as all members held a Forest membership.[1]

It wasn't a Shack, but it was a sanctuary. The building offered indoor bathrooms, heat and air-conditioning, a refrigerator and microwave, and—perhaps most importantly—no grounds work, hauling in wood, or maintenance. There was even space to store the club's tables and cabinets. With chairs arranged and coffee brewing, the clubhouse spirit flickered back to life. Members gathered, laughed, and lingered, surrounded by the quiet beauty of the wetlands and the winding Gifford Memorial Boardwalk, which led to a two-story tower overlooking the Great Marsh.[1]

*Clubhouse #5 on move-in-day in 2014 * photo courtesy of Thomas Rubarth*

The Wetlands Learning Center, opened in 1999, had been designed for education and reflection. For the Omaha Walking Club, it became a place of renewal. Though the building wasn't theirs, it felt like home—warm and welcoming.[19]

But nature, ever unpredictable, had one final chapter to write. On March 2, 2019, the club met there for the last time. A powerful flood swept through the forest lowlands, cresting high enough to breach the raised building and submerge the floor by nearly two feet. The damage was devastating. The Wetlands Learning Center was deemed beyond repair. Fontenelle Forest made the difficult decision to tear down the structure. For the first time in nearly a century, the Omaha Walking Club had no gathering place. To make matters worse, some of the club's memorabilia—precious fragments of its long and lively history—were lost to the water. Clubhouse #5 was the last in the club's long history, each shaped by generosity and resilience.[1]

Shelter in Spirit

Despite the absence of walls and roof, the essence of the club endures. Members gather on trails and in parks. What had once lived in timber now lives in tradition. The lack of a physical clubhouse reminds the walkers of what truly matters—not the building, but the people, the path, and the stories told beneath any sky.

To this day, the club continues its hikes and celebrations without a permanent home, carrying forward a legacy built on resilience and the unwavering belief that community needs no roof to flourish.

Final photo of clubhouse #5 in March 2019 before the flood
Photo courtesy of Thomas Rubarth

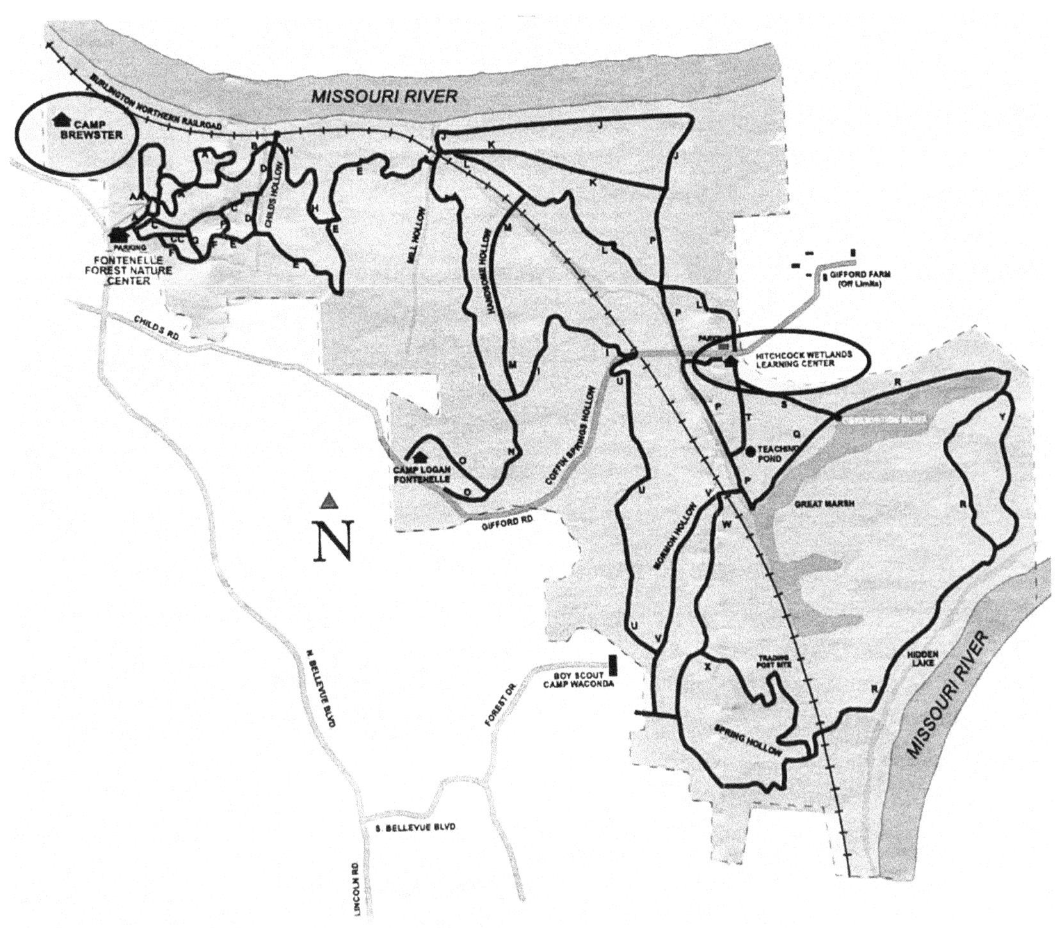

Trail map from about 2012 showing the sites of the final two clubhouses. Camp Brewster is circled near the top of the map, and the Hitchcock Wetlands Learning Center is circled near the east border of Fontenelle Forest by the entrance to Gifford Farm.

Chapter 4:
Getting There & Getting the Word Out

In 1919, members of the Omaha Walking Club met at streetcar junctions and had walk schedules printed in bulletins and in the newspaper. Over the following century, the rhythms of walking life adapted to an evolving world—one shaped by expressways, suburban sprawl, and digital communication. This chapter explores the shifting ways club members have stayed connected and moved through their world, from boarding trains with paper tickets to coordinating weekend hikes via text. Over the decades, the club's methods of transportation and communication transformed—but the spirit of gathering to walk remained remarkably steady.

From Steel Rails to Steering Wheels

In the early 1900s, Omaha's streets hummed to the click-clack of electric trolleys. Private companies laid miles of overhead wire, linking downtown Omaha to booming suburbs in each direction. By 1919, the city boasted many miles of streetcar routes, making transit affordable and reliable for the public. This network set the stage for club founders to trade city sidewalks for forest paths without owning a horse or automobile.

Beyond city limits, interurban railroads bridged Omaha to neighboring towns and countryside shrines. Passenger trains transported the Walking Club to other destinations in eastern Nebraska and western Iowa. These steel arteries drew walkers out of urban doldrums and into Nebraska and Iowa's natural splendor.

As the years went on, buses began to replace streetcars, and maintenance of aged tracks waned. The last Omaha trolley clanged its final run in 1955, while freight rails

*"Streetcar by Henry Hamann" 1951 * From the KMTV/Bostwick-Frohardt Photo Collection, permanently housed at The Durham Museum*

survived only for industrial sidings. Members mourned the loss of their beloved trolleys yet discovered new freedom in flexible schedules and off-grid trailheads once unreachable by rail.

The 1952 Yearbook had the following article giving advice to members who didn't have cars called "Take The Bus":

> If you haven't been coming down to the Shack for lack of transportation, try the bus from the 16th & Jackson Bus Station down the highway to the Camp Brewster Road. Florence and Sharkey say it is a fast trip and that it takes only ten more minutes to walk to the Donut House. Buses still leave 24th & N going down the boulevard at 10:30 a.m. and 12:30 noon but if you can't make it that soon, take a bus at 16th & Jackson at 1:50 or 3:10 p.m. Coming home you can get a bus below Camp Brewster at 4:20; 5:30; 7:00 or 8:35 p.m.

Crossing the Big Muddy

In the early days of the club, crossing the Missouri River was often inconvenient. Members from the Iowa side had to make the journey west for most events, and the club itself had to venture east whenever a walk was scheduled in Iowa. But with few bridges in place, the river posed a real logistical challenge.

The Plattsmouth Bridge didn't arrive until 1929, replacing a ferry service. The South Omaha Bridge followed in 1934,[34] making the Bellevue ferry obsolete. The Bellevue Bridge wouldn't be built until 1950, and the Mormon Bridge in north Omaha came even later, in 1952.[35]

Before these crossings existed, club members got creative. They often used Omaha's existing bridges, but when those weren't practical, they took ferries, paddled across in canoes, or—when winter cooperated—walked over the frozen river itself. Getting there wasn't always easy, but it was part of the adventure.

Newspapers & Website Notices

The Omaha Walking Club published its first Bulletin in 1919. The club still publishes a printed Bulletin every two months, listing upcoming walks and club news. In the early years, the scheduled walks were also printed in the newspapers as outreach to the public, but now the walks are posted on the club's website. While local newspapers no longer carry the schedule, this dual approach of print and online ensures every member knows where to gather each week.

The Roads We've Taken

From ferries and frozen crossings to bridges and broadband, the club has always found a way forward. What began with streetcars and newspaper notices now continues through car rides and website updates—proof that the spirit of walking, gathering, and exploring adapts with the times. The roads we've taken may look different, but the destination remains the same: connection, community, and the joy of the journey.

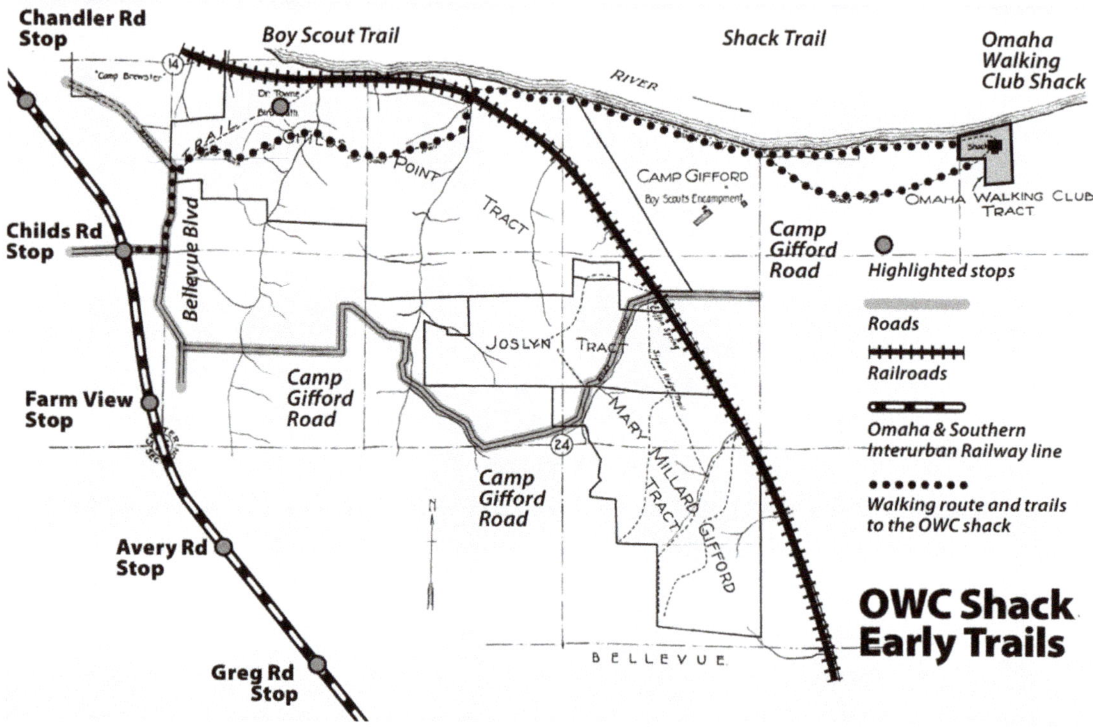

This map shows the interurban railcar route most early Walking Club members would have taken to reach Fontenelle Forest. After their stop, they would climb the hill to Camp Brewster (upper left on map), then walk several doors down to the entrance of the forest. After entering the forest, they would descend the hill and cross the railroad tracks, passing by the 100-acre Boy Scout Camp Gifford. Then they would follow one of the trails next to the Missouri River to reach the club's grounds. See Omaha Streetcar Map In APPENDIX C for a wider view of the early transportation system.

Map courtesy of Thomas Rubarth

Chapter 5:
Faces of the Footpath – Member Profiles

The Omaha Walking Club's story unfolds through its people. Each member carries unique motivations, challenges, and triumphs that enrich the century-long journey. Their faces—etched by sun, wind, and determination—become living landmarks on every trail.

The club has always been a mixture of men and women. In the beginning, most of the members were young to middle-aged. As the years passed and early members aged, there were senior citizens in the mix along with new members who were often very young.

Founders on the Trail

Before the club had a name, a logo, or a single scheduled walk, it had an idea—and a few passionate people willing to take the first step. This section honors the original minds and hearts behind the club, whose vision turned casual strolls into a lasting legacy.

Although Edwin Jewell was called the "father of the Omaha Walking Club," he gave the credit for the club's founding to four women. The stories of these five founders follow.

Edith Tobitt – Library Director, Co-Founder & First President

Born in January 1868[36] in England, Edith Tobitt arrived in Omaha with her parents in 1873. She had a deep love of literature and landscape. Her early years instilled a belief that books and nature were twin sources of inspiration.

As director of the Omaha Public Library from 1898 to 1934, Tobitt oversaw the growth of the main library and the addition of four branches.[37] When the Omaha Walking Club formed in 1919, she was chosen its first president.

In 1924, the Omaha World-Herald placed her on its celebrated "The Men Who Built Omaha" list, a testament to her transformative civic vision (and a nod to her trailblazing spirit).[38] Through decades of library innovations and forest excursions, Edith

*Edith Tobitt * From the collections of Omaha Public Library*

Tobitt embodied the club's twin pursuits of discovery and community—her legacy woven into every path and page.

Mrs. Helen Morton – Teacher, Co-Founder & First Secretary

Born in Omaha in May 1885,[36] Helen Hendrie Morton brought both vision and vitality to the early years of the Omaha Walking Club. A graduate of the University of Nebraska and a dedicated teacher at South High School, she served as

*Helen Morton with George on wedding trip in 1916 * courtesy of Steven Morton*

Junior Class sponsor and chaperoned a hiking club for young people—planting the seeds of lifelong appreciation for nature and fellowship.[39]

Helen was 33 when the Omaha Walking Club was founded, and she quickly became a guiding force. Alongside her husband, **George T. Morton**, she helped shape the club's spirit of adventure and community. George, a widower[40] before marrying Helen in 1916, was 41 at the time of the club's founding[36]. He was known for his active participation in walks and trips, his service as a club officer, and his famously good coffee[4] brewed for weary hikers.

Their personal journey was marked by both sorrow and strength. Just two months before the club's founding, Helen and George lost their first child, a baby boy born in January 1919 who died the next day. They welcomed two more sons in 1920 and 1922,[41] and despite the demands of young parenthood, the Mortons remained deeply involved in club life—including a memorable trip to the Big Horn country in 1926.[42]

Beyond the club, George Morton was a pioneer in Omaha's civic development. He was instrumental in establishing the City Planning Commission and served as its first chairman. He developed the Morton Meadows and Harrison Heights neighborhoods[43] and later became a trustee of the Fontenelle Forest Association,[19] further cementing the family's legacy in shaping Omaha's natural and urban landscapes. In addition to George serving on the Fontenelle Forest board,[44] the Mortons donated 10 acres of land to the forest in 1940.[19]

Helen Morton's early leadership helped define the club's inclusive and adventurous spirit. Her blend of intellect, warmth, and commitment to community made her a foundational figure in the club's history—and a model for generations of walkers to come.

Allie Houston – Trail Leader, Co-Founder & First Treasurer

Allie Houston was 37 years old[36] when she sparked the Omaha Walking Club's very first outing in March 1919—making the telephone calls that brought the inaugural group together. By day, she worked as a bookstore clerk, a role that sharpened the precision and patience she would later bring to her club duties. Elected as the club's first treasurer, Houston managed dues, expenses, and donations with quiet competence and care.[1]

But her talents extended far beyond the ledger. Known for her stamina and spirit, Allie regularly led hikes and inspired fellow members with her energy and enthusiasm. In 1921, she was elected club president, a recognition of her leadership and deep commitment to the club's growth.[1]

That same year, a local newspaper columnist spotted her boarding the Florence streetcar in khaki knickers, a coat, and a green hat. "Graceful and pretty as she looks," the columnist wrote, "they say she can do a dog trot around most of the men…" It was a fitting tribute to a woman who combined elegance with endurance.[45]

Allie didn't just lead walks—she climbed mountains. In 1921, she reached the summit of Long's Peak, Colorado's highest mountain, during one of the club's extended vacation trips.[46] Her adventurous spirit and

Allie wore old army "wraps" as leg protection on hikes

steady presence made her a beloved figure in the club's early years.

Allie remained an active member for decades, still part of the club during its 50th anniversary.[16] Her legacy lives on in every well-planned hike, every shared trail, and every moment when leadership meets laughter on the path.

Mrs. Isabel Robbins – Social Reformer & Club Co-Founder

At 48 years old,[36] Mrs. Isabel Robbins was one of four women credited with launching the walking club in 1919. With a simple idea and a shared love of walking, she helped spark a movement that would endure for generations.

Beyond the trails, Robbins was deeply committed to her community. She was active in Omaha's Social Settlement, an organization devoted to helping immigrant families adjust to life in America.[47] Her work reflected a spirit of inclusion and compassion that carried into her role in the club.

The Robbins family embraced the walking club as a shared pursuit. Her husband, **John W. Robbins**, a respected realtor and Nebraska state senator, was also a member, as were their daughters **Lois**, **Polly**, and **Dean**. In time, daughter Lois would marry fellow club member **Leo Bozell**,[54] weaving the club's legacy into the fabric of Omaha's civic and social life.

Mrs. Robbins' early leadership helped shape the club's welcoming, community-minded ethos. Her legacy lives on in every step taken with purpose, and in the enduring belief that a simple walk can bring people together.

Edwin "Pops" Jewell – "Father of the Omaha Walking Club"

Affectionately known as "Pops," Edwin S. Jewell was 51 years old[36] when he joined the founding circle of the Omaha Walking Club in March 1919. A former member of the Prairie Club in Chicago,[3] Jewell brought with him a deep appreciation for organized outdoor recreation and a wealth of experience that helped shape the Omaha club's early structure and spirit. His influence was so profound that he was often referred to as the "father of the Omaha Walking Club."[1]

A building manager by trade, Jewell oversaw several properties in Omaha before taking on the role of manager at the newly built Joslyn Memorial Museum in 1931.[48] His professional skills translated seamlessly into club life—he was a master organizer, instrumental in growing the club's membership and coordinating its many activities.

Jewell's leadership extended beyond city limits. In the club's early years, he led members on multi-week expeditions to the Rocky Mountains, fostering camaraderie and a love for rugged adventure.[3] On one such trip, a pristine lake in Rocky Mountain National Park was named in his honor. Jewell Lake remains a quiet tribute to the man who encouraged countless walkers to explore both trail and terrain.[1]

At the time of his death in 1941, Jewell was serving on the board of the Fontenelle Forest Association,[49] continuing his lifelong commitment to nature and community. His legacy lives on in every well-planned hike, every shared campfire, and every member who finds joy in the journey.

"Edwin S. Jewell - Portrait at desk" 1931-12-29 From the KMTV/Bostwick-Frohardt Photo Collection, permanently housed at The Durham

Stepping Up: Other Early Influencers

While the founders sparked the idea, many other early members helped give it momentum. Their enthusiasm, creativity, and diversity helped shape the Omaha Walking Club's culture, turning a fledgling concept into a thriving community. This section features some of the interesting individuals who helped shape the club in those formative years.

Dr. Harold Gifford Sr. – Ophthalmologist & Club Benefactor

Born in Milwaukee in 1858, Dr. Harold Gifford Sr. brought both medical brilliance and a deep love of nature to Omaha. A pioneering ophthalmologist and respected community leader, he was also a passionate conservationist whose love of nature helped shape the early identity of the walking club.[20]

In the spring of 1919, Gifford led some of the club's earliest walks, including a memorable outing to Wiley Point on April 20.[3] His deep knowledge of botany and ornithology made him a treasured guide, and his enthusiasm for the natural  world was infectious. The following year, he transformed the club's informal weekend rambles into something more enduring by donating a three-room house nestled deep in the forest. This gift became the club's first true home—a place for meals, music, planning, and shelter from the elements.[1]

Gifford's generosity extended far beyond the trails. He donated to both Fontenelle Forest[19] and Gifford Park and made significant contributions to Methodist Hospital. He was also involved in the Scouts, Camp Gifford, and the Camp Brewster YWCA. His legacy in Omaha's civic and environmental life was as lasting as his medical achievements.[50]

Though he remained an active member through most of the 1920s, he was later honored with lifetime membership in recognition of his contributions. Dr. Gifford passed away on November 28, 1929, leaving behind a legacy defined by healing eyes and nurturing spirits—both in the clinic and in the woods.[3]

Dr. Gifford

Jim Baldwin – WWI Veteran, Outdoorsman & Forest Storyteller

Jim Baldwin was in his early thirties when he joined the club soon after it was formed.[36] After serving as an infantryman in World War I,[51] he eventually became a small farmer with his father and brother. Their little farm and the shack they lived in bordered the southern edge of Fontenelle Forest. In his old age, Baldwin would later become locally famous as the "Hermit of Fontenelle Forest," welcoming groups of children to his simple abode to spin stories and tall tales.[19] He was also a voracious reader and would accept any reading material people would give him.[1] But before this stage of his life, he was a very active member of the Omaha Walking Club.

An exceptional outdoorsman, Jim led countless long-distance hikes, guiding novices through hidden ravines and creek beds. For years in the 1920's, he hosted large New Year's Eve's parties at the Shack, lantern-lit feasts—complete with music, fun, and laughter echoing through the trees. He also served as lifeguard for the club.[3] On the Missouri River, his canoe journeys stretched many miles, sometimes over days or weeks. He was also very handy with maintenance and building projects at the club's shack.

Although he was a valuable member of the club, his clothing sometimes left something to be desired. The Omaha Daily News ran a story on this called "Jim Now Can Swim" on February 20, 1927:

Jim Baldwin in 1923 * photo by Bill Coons, courtesy of Fontenelle Forest

Jim Baldwin, a long, tall, drink-o'-water, over six feet, blonde and rangy, is a great walker. He'll walk in any kind of weather, in any kind of garb. Needless to say, he's a member of the Omaha Walking Club.

Jim may be known for his walking among all his friends, but at the walking club shack in Fontenelle Forest he was known for his rather ventilated (moth-eaten) bathing suit. The suit has been the fear of many lady members of the walking club, and they are in the great majority.

So, the board of directors of the walking club took up the matter of Jim's bathing suit.

There was much discussion, pro and con. Finally, the board sent Jim an official letter, telling him to equip himself with a bathing suit not quite so holey, or else keep to his khaki breeches around the shack.

That made Jim's friends mad.

But not Jim.

For he was the recipient, in the next few days, of eight bathing suits!

Jim's sister Nell and brothers John and Julius ("Jack") were also members of the Omaha Walking Club in the early years.[3]

Nell Baldwin – Trail Leader, Cook & Songstress

Nell Baldwin was in her mid-twenties[36] when she joined the club. A sister of Jim, John, and Julius Baldwin, she quickly wove herself into the club's fabric with equal parts warmth and daring.

Nell guided countless hikes—through forests and wildflower meadows—with a steady voice and an encouraging laugh.[3] When not on the trail, her hearty stews were appreciated at many meals. She led singalongs and organized communal meals that turned strangers into friends.[1]

An accomplished swimmer like her brother Jim, Nell tackled the Missouri River's currents with confidence. In the summer of 1930, she and club member Esther Robinson embarked on a pioneering canoe journey from Omaha to Kansas City. Over a number of adventurous days and nights, they navigated shifting channels, portaged around sandbars, and camped in a tent—solidifying Nell's reputation as both a skilled athlete and a spirited explorer.[52]

*Nell Fixing Grub * World-Herald, June 1, 1930*

Through leading over trails, cooking pots, and song sheets, Nell left an indelible mark on the club.

Leo Bozell – WWI Veteran, Newspaper Editor & Advertising Pioneer

Leo Bozell joined the club soon after its formation in 1919. At 32 years old,[36] he was a World War I veteran[53] and recent widower,[51] seeking solace in sunrise hikes and forest camaraderie. His steady presence and frequent leadership on the trail quickly earned the respect of fellow walkers.

Before the war, he was an editor at the Omaha Daily News, then spent several years in real estate.[53] In 1921, he co-founded the advertising and public relations firm Bozell & Jacobs, drawing on his entrepreneurial drive and communication skills. The agency's pro bono work in the 1930s helped bring national attention to Boys Town, and the company continued to operate under the Bozell name more than a century later.[20] His background in media and outreach was valuable to the club's visibility and growth.

Leo Bozell * from Lois Bozell's journal, courtesy of Nebr. State Historical Society

Leo was active in many civic organizations and served as a trustee of Fontenelle Forest,[49] deepening his ties to Omaha's natural and cultural life. Somewhere along the way—whether through the club or long before—he met **Lois Robbins**, daughter of founding members **Mr. and Mrs. John Robbins**. Lois was a swimming instructor at Camp Holliday, and their shared love of long hikes led to the club's first engagement in 1920. They married the following summer in a ceremony witnessed by eighty Camp Fire Girls.[54]

Lois Robbins * from Lois' journal, courtesy of Nebr. State Historical Society

Together, Leo and Lois Bozell helped shape both the personal and organizational legacy of the Omaha Walking Club. Their story—rooted in resilience, community, and shared adventure—still echoes in every step taken along the trails they once walked.

Edith Neale – Educator, Historian & Philanthropist

Born in Washington County, Nebraska, in 1891,[36] Edith Neale devoted her life to education, conservation, and the preservation of local history. A graduate of the University of Nebraska in 1914, she later earned a master's degree from the University of Chicago.[55]

In 1923, Edith and her older sisters, Grace and Bertha, joined the Omaha Walking Club and were members for several years.[3] That same year, the trio traveled with the club to Glacier National Park in Montana, embracing the spirit of adventure and camaraderie.[56] Edith later became active with the club again by leading walks near Fort Calhoun in 1934[57] and 1935.[58] Even in her later years, she could still outpace hikers decades her junior, navigating the hills and valleys near her home with ease.[59]

Her impact extended far beyond the trail. In 1971, Edith donated 120 acres of land her father had homesteaded in the mid-1800s, creating what is now Neale Woods—a sanctuary for public enjoyment and ecological study just north of Omaha. That gift, paired with an additional 60 acres donated by Carl Jonas, brother-in-law to Dr. Hal Gifford Jr., helped preserve a vital piece of Nebraska's natural heritage.[19]

Edith was named the first director emeritus of Fontenelle Forest, a reflection of her enduring commitment to conservation. She also co-founded the Fort Atkinson Foundation and served as director of the Washington County Museum until 1971, leading restoration efforts and curating exhibits that celebrated pioneer life.[59] Her work inspired generations to value Nebraska's cultural and ecological legacy.

Edith Neale's life was a testament to quiet leadership, fierce dedication, and the belief that history and nature are best preserved by those who walk them with purpose.

*Edith Neale * photo courtesy of Washington County Museum*

Collective Legacy

These faces of the footpath represent the walking club at its best: a tapestry of courage, curiosity, diversity, and creativity. Their stories echo with shared laughter beneath oak canopies and the everyday acts that sustain community. Through them, the club's heartbeat remained vibrant—every step a tribute to those who came before and an invitation to those yet to lace their shoes.

Chapter 6:
Walking Together & Expanding Horizons

In the spring of 1919, most members of the newly formed Omaha Walking Club lived in the city and relied on streetcars to reach the starting points of their weekly hikes. The rhythm of the rails shaped the rhythm of the walks—departure times varied depending on the streetcar schedule, and the meeting spots were often chosen for their proximity to the end of a line.

Each Sunday brought a new destination and a fresh adventure. The club wandered through the wooded hills of Florence, the river-view bluffs of Iowa, and the quiet groves of Child's Point. Some walks meandered through farmland or blossoming orchards, offering a pastoral counterpoint to the city's bustle.

*87 members on walk to Iowa orchard country in the rain * May 18, 1919*

From the very beginning, the walks were numbered—a tradition that continues to this day. The first dozen hikes of spring 1919 spanned all directions, from the forests of Bellevue to the orchards of Council Bluffs.[60] Each walk had a designated leader, a scheduled start time, and a distinct character—some marked by mud, and many by laughter and camaraderie.[3]

Walk #1: The inaugural walk on March 30, 1919, set the tone for what would become a tradition of spirited exploration. Led by **Edith Tobitt**, one of the club's founding members, the group gathered at the end of the Albright streetcar line and ventured into Fontenelle Forest. There, beside a crooked highway and atop a fallen tree, the Omaha Walking Club was officially organized. Twenty-four walkers made the journey to Coffin Springs, marking the beginning of a legacy rooted in nature, camaraderie, and a touch of whimsy.

Walk #2: The following week, on April 6, Bess Dumont—a gym teacher at Central High School—led a walk from downtown Omaha to Mynster Springs in Council Bluffs. The day was memorable not only for its scenic route but for the dramatic backdrop in the sky: the Dundee tornado struck that same afternoon. Thirty-two members walked under unsettled skies, their steps echoing the unpredictability of spring.

Walk #3: April 13 brought the group north to Florence Park, where Margaret Colvin guided thirty-seven members to DeBolt (at the time a village near what is today Immanuel Hospital). Tornado wreckage from the previous week was still visible, lending a surreal quality to the walk. Nature's resilience—and the club's—was on full display.

Walk #4: On April 20, **Dr. Harold Gifford Sr.** led a nature walk through Fontenelle Forest that would prove foundational in more ways than one. Starting from the old Country Club crossing on the Fort Crook interurban line, the group passed through Camp Brewster, the bird preserve, and the Boy Scout grounds. Dr. Gifford, a passionate naturalist and philanthropist, spoke about trees, birds, and the Scouts' plans for the area. He also guided the club along the trail that would later lead to its permanent camp. That evening, coffee and sandwiches were served on the "river beach."[61]

Walk #5: Dr. Robert Fletcher Gilder led the club's walk on April 27 through Fontenelle Forest, guiding forty-seven members on a four-hour trek despite

Dr. Gilder

steady rain.[62] A journalist, self-taught archaeologist, and painter, Gilder had conducted digs in the forest years earlier, uncovering prehistoric village sites along the Missouri River bluffs. He had published his findings in the newspaper and professional journals. In later years, he would produce hundreds of landscape paintings that would become his legacy. On this walk, he pointed out Fontenelle's Grave and other archaeological landmarks, sharing stories of the land's deeper history. His passion for the forest—both as a place of scientific discovery and artistic inspiration—made the walk both educational and poetic.[63]

Walk #6: May brought longer days and larger crowds. On May 4, Lila Bowen led forty-nine members from Seymour Lake to Elmwood Park. The walk was long, the terrain varied, and by the end, "everybody had enough for one day."

Walk #7: The following Sunday, **Allie Houston**—another founding member— guided sixty-eight walkers from Horse Thief Cave to Copper Hollow starting at the end of the Florence streetcar line. It was dubbed "the beauty walk of the year," and rightly so.

Walks #8 and #9: Rain returned on May 18, when Jeannette McDonald led eighty-seven brave souls from Council Bluffs into Iowa orchard country via "The Sky Line." Everyone got a good wetting, but spirits remained high. On May 25, David Broadwell led a quieter walk through Bellevue, with thirty-five members in attendance.

Walks #10, #11, and #12: Lewis Whitehead's walk to Lake Manawa on June 1 was "known as the mud walk," and only fifteen members showed up to slosh through it. The next week's walk to the Pottawattamie Trail was postponed due to weather, but Margaret Flickinger still led thirty-two members on this outing. The final walk of the season, on June 15, was a scorcher. Mary Bourke led thirty members to Carter Lake, where the heat was so intense it earned a simple, emphatic review: "Hot—Hot—Hot."

After pausing the walks in the summer, the Omaha Walking Club resumed its outings in the fall of 1919, with renewed energy and a growing roster of leaders.

Walk #13: Margaret Flickinger led seven walkers southeast from the end of the streetcar line in Council Bluffs to Mosquito Creek on September 21. The country was rolling, the trail winding and scenic.

Walk #14: On September 28, fourteen walkers under the guidance of Mr. and Mrs. Oscar Williams started in Florence, then headed north along the River Road to Ponca Creek and Big Spring. It was remembered as the "day of the courthouse riot."

Walk #15: Hattie Mueller welcomed forty-eight walkers to Iowa Lake on October 5. "Those who were late found those who were on time at Mynster Spring."

Walk #16: Corinne Armstrong led seventy-seven walkers from the Florence streetcar line to Long's Hill on October 12. "This was the time the farmer's wife chased the apple stealers."

Walk #17: Despite the rain on October 19, **Leo Bozell** led thirty-seven walkers to Child's Point. "It rained but only one missed seeing the Point."

Walk #18: Mr. and Mrs. R. E. Winkleman led forty-four walkers from the Florence streetcar line to Briggs on October 26.

Walk #19: November 2 brought thirty-nine walkers together under the leadership of C. S. Stebbins. Starting from the Benson streetcar line, they headed north to Military Avenue, which is said to be the route of the old Oregon Trail.

Walk #20: Only seven walkers braved the rain on November 9, joining Mary Quigley for a walk that passed through Ak-Sar-Ben Field. It became "known as the rainy day walk."

Walk #21: Judge J. W. Woodrough led twenty-four walkers on a brisk 10-mile trek from Ralston to Millard on November 16. "Judge Woodrough set up some extra fine coffee and cake."

Walk #22: Leon O. Smith's November 23 walk from Avery to Fort Crook via College Hill, was meant to be longer, but the walk was "called at Harriet McMurphy's forest home." Fifty-three attended.

Walk #23: City Commissioner **Roy N. Towl** led eighteen walkers through the Fontenelle Reserve to the south terminus of his proposed River Boulevard on November 30. Although guided by the man who originated the idea for the River Boulevard, "Commissioner Roy Towl made a speed record for the club."

Walk #24: On December 7, Zaidee Dorsey led twenty-two determined walkers through Benson Gardens. "Snow very deep; coal very scarce; street cars thirty minutes apart."

Walk #25: Grant Cleveland led thirteen walkers through East Omaha and the Big Missouri River Hump on December 14. It was "known as the ice walk."

Walk #26: On December 21, A. E. Groetchel led thirteen walkers through Mandan Park, down a slippery hill along the Burlington tracks to Coffin Spring. "This walk was through a frost fairyland."

Walk #27: The final walk of the year took place on December 28, 1919, when G. Seaberg led eleven walkers through the Iowa Triangle, starting in Council Bluffs.

As 1919 came to an end, the Omaha Walking Club reflected on its first steps—through heat, mud, frost, and deep snow. They were rained on, iced over, and once chased by a farmer's wife for swiping apples. By year's end, they'd covered miles, made memories, and proved that good shoes and good company could carry you far.

*Dr. Gifford Sr. with Muggings the dog (ca. 1925) * photo courtesy of Fontenelle Forest*

After that first year, Dr. Harold Gifford Sr. led several more walks in the years following the club's founding. In April 1920, he guided members from the Hillcrest station on the Bellevue and Fort Crook Interurban line through the southern edge of Fontenelle Forest. Along the way, the group observed native birds and visited historic Indian mounds—sites first brought to prominence by Dr. Gilder's archaeological discoveries. The route wound past Mormon Hollow, circled Herron Lake, and returned through Child's Woods. That October, Dr. Gifford led another walk through the southern forest, and in June 1921, he was once again at the helm for a summer outing.[3]

In 1921, following the establishment of the club's headquarters near the eastern border of Fontenelle Forest, Saturday afternoon walks were introduced. These informal hikes offered members an additional opportunity to explore the woods, socialize, and enjoy the changing seasons. The route often began at the end of the Albright streetcar line winding past Camp Brewster and into the forest along well-loved trails. Whether taking the full six-mile round trip or shortening the journey via the Bellevue and Fort Crook interurban, walkers embraced the ritual with enthusiasm. Reaching the Shack was a hike in itself—an initiation into the club's ethos of movement, nature, and community.[1]

The forest offered a changing canvas with each season. In winter, the trails were hushed under snow. Spring brought carpets of ferns and wildflowers. Summer shaded the path with a canopy of green, and autumn turned the woods into a rustling blaze of color.

Directions for getting to the Shack were printed in the club's Saturday Walk schedule in 1921:

> The route will be along Bellevue Boulevard past Camp Brewster a short distance, to the entrance of Fontenelle Forest. The walk through the forest will be over what is known as "White Trail" (the favorite route of the Boy Scouts) to the Burlington Railroad. After crossing the Burlington tracks the walk will continue along one of the trails that parallel the river until the big boat is reached. From this point walkers will follow the trail along the river across the clearing into the woods, thence southeast to the barbed wire fence, thence east along the fence to "the path the calf made." "The path the calf made" leads directly to the Omaha Walking Club Camp and Club House.

On the way to the Shack, members usually passed a spot affectionately known as the "Donut House." In the 1920s, Bessie Morgan[64]—fondly remembered as the "Donut Lady"—sold fresh donuts to Boy Scouts and Walking Club members from a cabin in the woods provided by Dr. Harold Gifford.[19] After her passing in 1930, the forest caretaker's family continued the tradition, offering donuts to hikers on Sundays. Longtime member Doug Wenger recalled the house being near what is now the Raptor Center, back when there was no visitor center. "So," he noted, "this end of the trail and the parking was always referred to simply as the Donut House." Though a road did lead down to the Shack, it was reserved strictly for extenuating circumstances—walking was, after all, the point.

Bessie Morgan, the "donut lady" * photo courtesy of Fontenelle Forest

Moonlight, Music, and Sentimental Souls

Buoyed by the success of their Saturday hikes, the club expanded its calendar to include moonlight walks by flashlight, early-morning treks at dawn, and other seasonal adventures. These twilight outings added a touch of romance and mystery to the club's repertoire.[1]

One such moonlight hike took place in July 1923. Walkers gathered at 8:30 p.m. at the end of the Forest Lawn streetcar line and began their journey in the cemetery. From there, they headed north into the Florence woods and on to Copper Hollow, returning along the river road under the stars to the Florence streetcar.[65]

Another moonlight hike was described in a report by the walk leaders: "At 8:00 on Sunday evening, September 14, 1924, 44 sentimental souls under the leadership of Mr. and Mrs. Frank Leslie, met at Bellevue Station. The trail followed the car line for a short distance, then through the woods back to 16th

"Sunset on the Missouri"
1927 * OWC photo by Roy H. Jensen

Street and out onto the boulevard leading past the cemetery. At the top of the hill which commanded a view of the river both north and south, a grassy knoll served as an ideal lounging place for a sing and afforded a fine view of the big, round moon as it rose over the water. The night was perfect, and no one cried to go home…"[1]

Moonlight hikes remained a cherished tradition for decades, a reminder that the club's spirit wasn't bound by daylight. Whether under sun or stars, the Omaha Walking Club walked not just for exercise, but for joy, connection, and the quiet magic of shared paths.[1]

Expanding the Landscape

After that inaugural forest ramble, the walking club quickly outgrew its home woods. The city's electric streetcar and interurban lines opened up a world of possibilities, allowing members to explore beyond the streetcar routes. Sunday hikes became expeditions, with walkers assembling at streetcar stops, boots laced and ready for wherever the rails might lead.

"On Walk of May 8th"
*1927 * OWC photo by Rudolph Timmler*

On November 16, 1919, Judge J. W. Woodrough led one of the club's earliest long-distance treks—a ten-mile hike beginning at the Ralston Interurban station. It was a bold outing, reserved for seasoned walkers, and it marked a turning point in the club's appetite for challenge and exploration.[66]

Other favorite destinations included the countryside north of Florence, the Iowa countryside, and the rolling terrain near Papillion and Benson—then still a separate town. Each walk began with the rhythmic clatter of steel wheels and the hum of anticipation. The ride itself became part of the ritual, a shared experience that set the tone for the miles ahead.[1]

This reliance on public transit shaped the club's creativity. Point-to-point routes minimized backtracking and maximized discovery. The city's transit grid became a launchpad for adventure, and with each new stop, the club expanded not just its landscape—but its spirit.

Endurance Hikes

Whether across forests, prairies, river bluffs, or city blocks, long-distance hikes tested the club's spirit and stamina. These extended journeys—some lasting all day—pushed walkers to new physical and mental frontiers. From early sunrise departures to evening returns with tired smiles, each hike told its own story of perseverance, discovery, and camaraderie.

The walks—especially the endurance walks—were often challenging. This "Hikers Hammer" poem printed in 1925 showed some humorous frustration toward the club's walk leaders. In this playful tribute, R. B. Gray vents (and laughs) about the mishaps of walk leaders, from soggy trails to bad coffee.

"High Line Trail North of Council Bluffs"
*1925 * OWC photo by Fred Deakle*

THE [WALK] LEADERS OF THE O. W. C.

Gimme that hammer,
I want to knock
Walking Club leaders,
The whole dumb flock.

Wherever they've led
I've tramped with a smile,
Followed their rambles,
Mile after mile.

Some walk in circles,
Some lose the trail,
Some never start—
But always they fail.

They lead you in water,
Both freezing and hot,
Land you in snow-drifts,
Leave you to rot.

Hang you on fences,
Stuff you with dust;
I'm full of cuss words,
'Bout fit to bust.

Still I could love them,
Stifle my ire,
If only the morons
Could build a good fire.

Weary and freezing
We wait round the pot;
They fuss and they fidget,
But nothing gets hot.

When you're disgusted,
Rarin' to go,
Round comes the bucket,
Ready to flow.

One of the club's more ambitious outings took place in November 1920, when a determined group of walkers gathered at 7:30 a.m. in Omaha to catch a train to Calhoun—despite the rain. Led by Ed M. Kennedy and Charles Gadway, the group trekked 12 miles back to Florence through wet fields and muddy roads, breaking at noon for a campfire lunch at a welcoming farmhouse. The full adventure lasted eight hours and included a spirited mix of walkers: Irma Gross, Esther Thomas, Ellen Hamilton, Nell Baldwin, and Helen Duffy, along with Arthur Graham, R. B. Gray, James Baldwin, Edwin Jewell, Homer Pennock, Leslie Williams, Leo Bozell, and Lyman Williams. It was a day of grit, camaraderie, and soggy socks—proof that a little rain never dampened the club's enthusiasm for a good walk.[67]

"Walk No. 323—70th and Hamilton Streets" Dec. 26, 1926 * OWC photo by Sol Hodes

By 1922, a twelve-mile trek was no longer considered ambitious by seasoned club members. Alongside shorter Sunday strolls, the club began scheduling endurance hikes of 20 to 25 miles, paced briskly at three to three-and-a-half miles per hour with only a brief stop for lunch. The first hike of the year—a twenty-mile journey—set off at 10:00 a.m. from the north end of the Florence streetcar line, following Blair Ridge Road all the way to Blair. After a full day on foot, hikers boarded a train back to Omaha, tired but triumphant. The walk was organized and led by the club's dedicated walks committee.[68]

Several weeks after their first long trek of the year, the walking club tackled a second endurance hike in 1922—this time a 25-mile journey from Missouri Valley to Council Bluffs. The group, which included three women—Nell Baldwin, Mrs. Wilmot Woods, and Mrs. Leo Bozell—alongside fourteen men, boarded an 8:00 a.m. train to Missouri Valley and began walking at 9:15. They reached Loveland by 10:11, Honeycreek at 11:25, and stopped for a well-earned lunch in Crescent at 1:08, resting for an hour before continuing on. By 4:16 p.m., they arrived in Council Bluffs—making better time than expected. Notably, Nell Baldwin added six more miles to her day, walking from the end of the Albright streetcar line to the club Shack and back after the hike. Her extra steps were a quiet testament to the grit and spirit that defined the club's early walkers.[69]

Endurance walks faded from the club's calendar after the 1920s, taking a long hiatus before making a quiet comeback decades later. In 1969, the tradition was rekindled with a 16-mile trek south of Blair, led by none other than 85-year-old "Pops" Lazure. His leadership proved that age was sometimes no barrier to adventure—and that the spirit of long-distance walking still pulsed through the club's veins.[70]

Another endurance walk was held in 1974. Twenty-eight members began a 20-mile trek in the hills near Crescent, Iowa. It was a chilly rainy day, but eleven members went the entire distance.[71]

Some walks went far beyond the club's official calendar—and far beyond the expected. In late March 1926, member Minnie May of Omaha, formerly of Nemaha, Nebraska, set out on an extraordi-

Pops leading endurance walk in Washington County in 1969

nary 88-mile journey back to her hometown, accompanied by Boy Scout Gordon Quiller. They left Omaha on a Monday morning, reaching Plattsmouth by noon. Tuesday brought them to Union by 3 p.m., and by Wednesday at 11:30, they arrived in Nebraska City. On Thursday, they reached Auburn at 4 p.m., and finally, on Friday morning at 10:15, they walked into Nemaha—five days, five towns, and one unforgettable feat of endurance.[72]

Train Expeditions

As the club's confidence grew, so did its curiosity—and soon, the trails extended far beyond city limits. Regional railroads became the gateway to daylong excursions, whisking walkers to scenic destinations like the Nebraska state fishery (now Schramm Park) on the Platte River, the riverfront bluffs of Plattsmouth, and the arboretum and historic trails of Nebraska City.[73]

*"The Road East from Murray on the way to King Mountain" April 3, 1932 * OWC photo by Roy Jensen*

One memorable outing took place on May 21, 1922, when members boarded a Missouri Pacific passenger train to Union, Nebraska. From there, they hiked to Nebraska City, exploring Arbor Lodge and Morton Park before catching the evening train back to Omaha—tired, happy, and full of stories.[74]

Another ambitious trek made headlines in the Gretna Breeze Newspaper that October: "The Omaha Walking Club consisted of twenty-five 'hikers' passed through Gretna last Sunday. They were walking from Ashland to Papillion and seemed to be full of pep when passing through Gretna." The club's energy was contagious, and their routes—often spanning many miles or more—became legendary.[75]

To keep things fresh, planners often designed point-to-point hikes, starting at one transit terminus and ending at another. This clever use of streetcars and trains allowed walkers to cover new ground without retracing their steps. With every clattering rail and dusty mile, the club expanded its reach—and its reputation for turning ordinary Sundays into extraordinary adventures.

Different Strides, Shared Spirit

As membership grew, the club embraced a two-tiered approach to Sunday walks: Endurance Walks—sometimes stretching beyond 20 miles—catered to seasoned hikers craving a challenge, while Regular Walks offered shorter, more relaxed routes for newcomers and those preferring a gentler pace. This thoughtful balance of grit and welcome helped define the club's identity: adventurous, yet inclusive.[73]

The Walking Club's tradition of welcoming walkers of all abilities is still alive and well. Today, participants often split into two groups at the same trailhead—one taking on the full route, sometimes adding extra miles, while the other enjoys a shorter, more relaxed version. Though modern walks are gentler than the ambitious treks of the early years, the heart of the tradition endures: each member walks their own pace and path, yet all share the journey together.

"Moonlight on the River"
*1929 * OWC photo by J. E. Brill*

Sunrise, Starlight, and Midweek Miles

In the summer of 1921, the club added a flavorful twist to its outings: early morning breakfast walks. The first required members to arrive at the Albright streetcar station by 5:30 a.m., then trek across Fontenelle Forest to its eastern edge. There, under the canopy of trees, they built a campfire and cooked up a hearty spread of bacon, eggs, and coffee. The event was led by Jim Baldwin, who clearly knew how to pair a good walk with a great breakfast.[76]

Not to be outdone, another adventurous group took on a midnight-to-sunrise hike through the hills north of Council Bluffs, lured by the promise of breakfast at a scenic campsite. These walks weren't just about mileage—they were about atmosphere, camaraderie, and the thrill of walking when most of the world was asleep.[77]

Decades later, the rhythm shifted but the spirit remained. In the mid to late 1990s, members began gathering at the Fontenelle Forest Nature Center for Wednesday morning walks, a tradition that eventually expanded to Wednesday evenings in summer, offering a midweek dose of nature and connection.[73]

And in September 2008, the club joined thousands of pedestrians to christen the Bob Kerrey Pedestrian Bridge, walking across the Missouri River on its inaugural day.[78] From sunrise hikes to sunset strolls, the club has always found new ways to keep moving—together.

From Young Trailblazers to Seasoned Striders

The Omaha Walking Club has always welcomed walkers of all ages, but a few members stood out for pushing the boundaries of youth and age alike.

In March 1921, two 13-year-olds—**Dean Robbins**, daughter of founding members Mr. and Mrs. John Robbins, and **Burton Guckert**—were selected to lead a club walk. Described as "expert hikers with an utter disregard for beaten paths," they charted a bold route beginning at the Albright streetcar line, winding through Mandan Park, and heading south to the Jewell place. Their youthful energy and fearless navigation set a spirited tone for the club's walk.[79]

*Dean Robbins & Burton Guckert * 13-Year-Old Walk Leaders in 1921*

Decades later, the club found inspiration at the other end of the age spectrum. In 1969, **Charles "Pops" Lazure Sr**. joined the club at age 85 and promptly led Endurance Hike No. 15, the first of its kind since the 1920s. Thirty-three members began the trek from the Art Beck farm south of Blair, chatting through the first mile. By mile three, sore feet began to slow some walkers, but Pops pressed on with a brisk pace. A van trailed the group, picking up three who dropped out, while the rest reached 72nd Street and Highway 36 after five and a half hours. Pops, unfazed, declared he was ready for next year's hike.[70]

In 1974, the club honored Pops with a surprise 90th birthday party at the Shack—naturally, he hiked 2½ miles through the forest to attend. Nearly 100 members gathered to celebrate the man whose footsteps had already covered decades of Nebraska soil. A graduate of the University of Nebraska School of Agriculture, Pops had spent his life walking—behind plows, across fields, and sometimes 20 miles in a single day.[1]

During hikes, Pops often shared stories from his youth, including conversations with Native Americans who lived near his family's farm. He spoke of a time when horses and wagons ruled the roads, offering fellow walkers a living bridge between past and present. In 1979, the club awarded him lifetime membership—a fitting tribute to a man who never stopped moving forward.[80]

*Pops Lazure (in plaid shirt) * OWC photo*

Boots, Blisters, and a New Spirit

Gone were the days of leisurely strolls in polished shoes, dresses, and suits. As the Omaha Walking Club grew, so did its appetite for adventure. Members embraced a more rugged spirit—trading dress shoes for hiking boots, and Sunday strolls for mountain scrambles. What began as a social pastime evolved into a culture of grit, resilience, and a shared love for the trail's tougher terrain.

This humorous poem was read at the Annual Meeting in January 1922. Framed as a mock lament from a concerned parent, it playfully chronicles the transformation of a once-refined daughter—and eventually her father—under the influence of hiking culture. It captures the club's eccentric charm with wit and warmth. What begins as a protest ends, inevitably, in reluctant—and hilarious—acceptance.

THE EPIDEMIC

I greatly fear, my daughter dear,
This hiking never will do,
For I am not sure that I can endure
What the club has done to you.

Six months ago, as well you know,
I looked on you with pride;
But now poor thing, when visitors ring
I have to bid you hide.

In days gone by no girl could vie
With you for fine attire;
But now you prance in khaki pants
That smell of a brushwood fire.

Your delicate shoes were Number Twos
A few short weeks before;
But with hob-nailed kicks that are branded "Six"
You batter now my floor.

A hair-net's tough and strong enough
To guard against a breeze;
But it will not save a permanent wave
From cockle-burrs and trees.

Of old you'd sing some gentle thing,
Some sweet, romantic tune;
But now all night by the fire-light
You crouch and bay the moon.

And yet for a while I tried to smile
Though all my sky seemed black
Till you took your dad (he was all I had)
Away to the hikers' Shack.

Now what you do at that rendezvous
I cannot guess nor name,
But ever since then that best of men
Has not been quite the same.

* O.D.'s: Short for Olive Drab, the standard color of military-style hiking gear—practical, not fashionable.

Wrap Puttees: Long cloth strips wrapped around the lower legs, once used by soldiers and hikers to protect against brush, mud, and cold. Stylish? Not exactly.

The Trail Is Just the Beginning

From sunrise breakfasts to midnight hikes, endurance treks to forest rambles, the Omaha Walking Club has never been defined by a single path. Its walks have spanned generations, landscapes, and levels of ambition—led by teenagers with a taste for adventure and octogenarians with stories to share. Whether riding streetcars to trailheads or crossing rivers on foot, members have always found joy in motion and meaning in miles. And as new walkers lace up their shoes and join the journey, they carry forward a tradition built not just on footsteps, but on friendship, curiosity, and the enduring thrill of discovering what lies just beyond the bend.

Chapter 7:
Gather, Laugh, Repeat

Long after the last boot was brushed off and the final mile tucked into memory, the Omaha Walking Club found its second wind—not on the trail, but around picnic tables, beside bonfires, and beneath the twinkling lights of the Shack. If hiking was the spine of the club, social gatherings were its soul: spontaneous, spirited, and stitched with laughter.

Doug Wenger, whose family's ties to the club stretch back to the 1930s, summed it up best at the centennial celebration: "Those people really knew how to have fun!" With no television and only a whisper of radio, members became their own entertainment committee—throwing elaborate costume parties, hosting talent shows, and square dancing to the scratchy tunes of a wind-up phonograph. One couple, Grace and Hoke Smith, even called square dances professionally, turning the Shack into a whirl of stomping boots.[13]

Annual traditions like Homecoming transformed the Shack into a stage for skits, games, and playful mischief—complete with a mock jail and imaginary infractions, all in good fun. And then there was the Shack Shower, a practical yet delightfully quirky ritual where members donated household items to keep the Shack stocked. Joe Burke's contribution of a shovel—"to stir the coffee"—was both useful and hilariously on-brand.[13]

From potlucks and hayrack rides to sledding at Winter Carnivals and impromptu singalongs under the stars, the club's social calendar was as lively as its hiking routes. Whether gathering at city parks, skating rinks, or members' backyards, these events offered more than just recreation—they built a community. Thick skin was helpful, comedy was plentiful, and the memories? Unforgettable.[2]

Shack Celebrations & Meals

If the Omaha Walking Club had a second love after walking, it was food—preferably cooked over open flames and served with strong coffee. Meals weren't just sustenance; they were events. Whether prepared in the Shack's cozy kitchen, over a firepit in Fontenelle Forest, or beside a campfire on the trail, food brought members together in delicious, memorable ways.

Spaghetti feeds, steak fries, and pancake breakfasts became cherished traditions. On weekends, Judge Charles E. Foster would swap his courtroom robes for khakis and hiking boots, trekking into the forest with a knapsack and a mission: to grill steaks over a wood fire and brew coffee for the club. After serving the meal, he'd clean up the Shack himself—earning high praise from Mrs. Helen Morton, who quipped, "He's perfectly trained, girls, just ready for someone to appropriate."[81]

The annual "chickenfest" was another highlight, drawing over a hundred hungry hikers to the Shack for hot biscuits, baked potatoes, and Homer Pennock's legendary chicken dinner. With two large ranges inside and a park stove outside, the Shack transformed into a bustling kitchen, filled with the scent of roasting meat and the hum of voices.[82]

Isabel Zigmund, Bess Turynek, Miss Poprosky, & Celeste McCurdy preparing to make dinner
Photo courtesy of Doug Wenger

And then there were the pancake feeds—"all you can eat" affairs where men took charge of the griddle. Earl Johnson, one of the masterminds behind the tradition, flipped flapjacks for two straight hours in March 1938, feeding sixty grateful members and likely earning hero status in the process.[83]

"New Outdoor Oven on Campground"
*1925 * OWC photo by S. N. Hodes*

The club's culinary creativity wasn't limited to the menu—it extended to the marketing. In the 1952 Membership Roster, members were invited to a "Free Reducing Course," cheekily aimed at gals who'd "picked up a few pounds during the winter." The program? No charge for grabbing one end of the crosscut saw on Sunday afternoons to help saw stove wood. The catch? After hauling it in and firing up the stove, you'd likely cook enough food to gain back everything you'd just burned off. Efficiency, humor, and hearty appetites—all in one workout.

Whether flipping flapjacks, roasting chicken, or brewing coffee strong enough to stir with a shovel, the Omaha Walking Club knew how to feed both body and spirit. These food events weren't just about nourishment—they were about camaraderie, tradition, and joy that lingers long after the dishes are done.

Singing Traditions

In the early decades of the club, melody was as much a part of the journey as the miles themselves. Whether striding through wooded trails, gathered in the Shack,

*Omaha Walking Club Group Photo in March 1941 * photo courtesy of Doug Wenger*

or circling a campfire under the stars, members often broke into song—familiar tunes that everyone seemed to know by heart. And if memory failed, the club's printed songbook was never far from reach, tucked into backpacks or passed from lap to lap like a treasured heirloom. Among the favorites was a piece known simply as "The Camper's Song" (source unknown), a lyrical tribute to the club's spirit of carefree adventure and communion with nature:[1]

Follow the trail to the open air,
Alone with the hills and sky.
A pack on your back but never a care,
Letting the days slip by!

Healing fragrance of pines in the dark,
Glow from a camper's fire,
Starlight and shadow and music of waves
While the grey smoke curls higher.

Follow the trail to the open air
Letting the day slip by,
A smile on your lips, a song in your heart
One with the hills and the sky.

It was more than a song—it was a philosophy, echoing through the forest and across generations.

Seasonal Traditions

In its early decades, the Omaha Walking Club didn't just mark the seasons—they celebrated them with gusto. The Shack's calendar filled quickly with festive parties and ambitious walks, each gathering a blend of homey comfort, hearty food, and the kind of camaraderie that made strangers into lifelong friends.

Autumn brought Halloween bonfires and treasure hunts through the forest, with stunts and laughter echoing under the trees. In 1926, 150 members and friends gathered at the Shack for a spirited celebration led by club president Earl Johnson.[84]

Thanksgiving offered a different kind of adventure in 1919. Members embarked on a full-day walk spanning over thirteen miles, fueled by hot baked potatoes and coffee prepared by Mrs. Helen Morton. University student Walter Wolff led the route, which wound through farms, parks, and creekside trails before ending at the Q streetcar line.[85]

Winter traditions were equally rich. Christmas parties welcomed members without family in town, offering warmth, a tree, and even a visit from Santa.[86] The club welcomed its very first New Year on January 1, 1920—not with champagne, but with a hike. Led by Leo Bozell, members met in Council Bluffs and trekked through deep ravines and high bluffs, rewarded with sweeping views of the Missouri Valley. Walking sticks were recommended, and while the route measured just six miles, the rugged terrain made it feel closer to ten. It was a brisk, scenic start to a tradition that would carry the club into many new years to come.[87]

In 1922, New Year's Eve was a highlight—members hiked to the Shack by moonlight then shared oyster stew at midnight. Jim Baldwin, who was also the caretaker of the Shack, was the host. On New Year's Day, the club returned for a bracing New Year's Day walk.[88] The following year, about 100 people celebrated New Year's Eve with Jim Baldwin hosting at the Shack again.[89]

*"Evening in February" 1924 * OWC photo by Rudolph Timmler*

Spring brought Easter egg-bakes and the promise of longer walks, while Memorial Day became a time for extended outings. In 1919, the club's first Memorial Day hike traced a twelve-mile loop from Plattsmouth to the historic town of Rock Bluff and back.[90]

Summer was a season of games and water fun. Fourth of July field days featured tennis, volleyball, horseshoes, canoe races, and swimming. The 1925 water carnival was a standout, turning the Shack into a hub of land and water activity.[91] These annual celebrations continued into the late 1920s, each one a joyful blend of movement, merriment, and memory-making.[92]

From bonfires to stew pots, treasure hunts to trail maps, the club's seasonal traditions stitched the year together. The walks may have varied, but the spirit remained the same: celebrate the moment and do it together.

Dances, Movies, & Other Outings

While the forest trails and Shack gatherings defined much of the Omaha Walking Club's identity, members also knew how to step out—literally. In the early decades, friendships forged on hikes found new rhythm on dance floors, theater aisles, and amusement park promenades.

Annual dances began in 1921, adding a touch of elegance to the club's calendar. The second, held at Hyland's Dancing Academy in February 1923, featured music by the Spinharney Orchestra. For those less inclined to dance, the balcony offered a lively card game alternative.[93] That same month, members walked ten miles to see The Golem at the Brandeis Theater—proving that even cinema outings could be earned one step at a time.[94]

Spring brought spontaneous joy, like the impromptu May-pole dance at the end of a hike in 1923, accompanied by a four-piece orchestra that also serenaded Sunday afternoons at the Shack.[95] A month later, members picnicked at Krug Park—then a bustling amusement park in Benson—before enjoying a swimming party and dancing under the stars, courtesy of the park's management.[96]

1931 Newspaper Ad

The club's sense of adventure extended to barn dances, ice-skating parties at Ak-Sar-Ben Coliseum,[97] and square dances at the Shack, which became official club activities in 1957.[1] Whether meeting at the Albright drug store to head to a barn dance in 1935[98] or gathering for a square dance in June 1956,[99] members embraced every opportunity to mix movement with merriment.

Even sports and city outings found their place. In 1957, seventeen members attended the Oregon-Nebraska football game in Lincoln, returning to Omaha by train and capping the day with dinner at the Rome Hotel.[100] More recently, the club's calendar has included movie nights and winery visits—proof that the spirit of recreation still thrives, even when the terrain is paved.

From dance halls to dining rooms, the Omaha Walking Club's off-trail traditions added rhythm and a touch of sparkle to its legacy—reminding everyone that the journey didn't end when the hike did.

Board Games & Pastimes

Board games became a staple at the clubhouse, especially for members who could no longer tolerate long walks. After the loss of the clubhouse, this tradition continued as an official activity at the Winter Walks & Games Day and is still a popular unofficial activity with some of the members. These tabletop contests deepened bonds as strategy and laughter intertwined.

Photo Frenzy

From its founding in 1919, the Omaha Walking Club embraced photography not just as a hobby, but as a way to preserve its spirit. In an era when box cameras like the Kodak Brownie were just becoming accessible to the public, members took to the trails with lenses in hand, determined to document every outing, campfire, and muddy boot.

In 1924 alone, the club's Photograph and Slides Committee compiled hundreds of images: 250 local activity shots, 93 from a mountain outing, and 70 from a "Gypsy Trip." They also produced 128 photographic lantern slides—bringing the total slide collection to 240. These images weren't just stored; they were celebrated. Annual contests awarded prizes for the best photos, with Rudolph Timmler and Sol N. Hodes taking top honors that year. Slide shows, dubbed "picture nights," used magic lanterns to project images onto walls, turning hikes into cinematic events. By 1927, moving pictures joined the mix.[3]

Members snapped hundreds of photos each year, often showcased in lively scrapbooks and slide shows. The club's albums and Hiker's Hammer volumes became treasured entertainment on stormy days—until the Shack fire tragically destroyed the collection. Yet, thanks to contributions from members and former members, many early photos were recovered, and the tradition of compiling photos continues to this day.[2]

Photography wasn't always easy. As walk leader Jennie Sharkey recalled in December 1924, "Mr. Timmler had us pose for a picture on Signal Hill with the wind blowing about sixty miles an hour. After two films had been spoiled and we became so chilled we were unable to move, he succeeded in getting the picture." Dedication, indeed.[1]

Among the club's many shutterbugs, at least two members turned their passion into professional careers.

Sol Hodes, joined the club around 1924 upon the advice of a doctor due to his bad health. After joining the club, he noticed the beauty of the outdoors and discovered a love for photography that led him to the pictorialist movement (a movement in the late 19th and early 20th century that elevated photography to an art). By 1930, his work was exhibited internationally—from Copenhagen to Chicago. Eventually, his artistic patience outpaced the club's walking pace, and he spent less time on hikes—waiting for perfect light wasn't always compatible with a brisk six-mile walk.[101]

*Sol Hodes * World-Herald, March 16, 1930*

Bill Coons, who joined the walking club in 1921, became a photographer for the Union Pacific Railroad in 1930.[102] He later became chief photographer in 1944. His scenic images graced calendars and publications for over three decades. He photographed Presidents Franklin Roosevelt, Harry Truman, and Dwight Eisenhower. He also photographed Hollywood stars such as Norma Shearer, Barbara Stanwyck, George Burns, and Gracie Allen.[103]

Bill & Inez Coons * photo courtesy of Sonja Hauter

Today, the photo tradition continues with smartphones and shared online galleries. Members now capture high-resolution shots of forest canopies, creek crossings, and group portraits—preserving each season's beauty with the same spirit that once filled Kodak albums and lantern slides. The tools may have changed, but the impulse remains: to hold onto the fleeting magic of a moment and share it with the people who helped make it unforgettable.

The Joy Between Journeys

Sometimes the deepest peace comes not from the trail, but from the fire after. This introspective poem was published in the 1969 Handbook:

When the wood has fallen low;
And the ashes start to whiten
Round the embers crimson glow;
Tell me were you ever nearer
To the land of heart's desire,
Than when you sat there thinking
With your feet before the fire?

-- R. L. STEVENSON

Between the miles and the memories, there was always room for joy. Whether gathered around a potluck table, belting out campfire tunes, or laughing through a board game, club members found connection in the spaces between the walks. Photo shows flickered with nostalgia, meals stretched into storytelling sessions, and music turned evenings into something magical. These gatherings weren't just entertainment—they were the heartbeat of the club, reminding everyone that the journey was richer when shared, and that joy, like a good trail, is best followed together.

Chapter 8:
Getting Away

From multi-week journeys in other states to weekend trips in closer locations, travel was a vital part of the Omaha Walking Club's spirit of exploration starting in the early 1920s. These trips—whether long or short—offered fresh landscapes, deeper camaraderie, and a chance to walk new paths together. This chapter explores some of these trips.

To Faraway Mountains and Lakes

Beginning in the 1920s, club members set their sights on landscapes beyond the Nebraska plains—venturing to mountain ranges and lakes that offered both challenge and serenity. These trips became cherished traditions, with groups traveling to the Black Hills, the Rockies, and the lake country of Minnesota and Wisconsin. Whether hiking alpine trails, camping beside quiet waters, or paddling through morning mist, members found renewal in these natural retreats. Over the decades, such journeys continued to draw walkers westward and northward, deepening their bond with the land and with one another.

1921 – Trailblazing in Rocky Mountain National Park:

In the summer of 1921, the walking club stretched its legs far beyond Nebraska, embarking on its first major western adventure—a two-week, 90-mile trek through Rocky Mountain National Park. Organized by Edwin Jewell, the trip marked a bold new chapter in the club's history, blending rugged exploration with the camaraderie that defined its earliest years.[46]

Ten members boarded a train to Denver, then traveled by automobile to the trailhead, where the real journey began. For fourteen days, they hiked through alpine meadows, forested valleys, and rocky passes, spending ten nights under canvas tents. The terrain was challenging, the scenery breathtaking, and the spirit of the group unwavering.[46]

Three members, Allie Houston, Maude Watson, and John Bath took the challenge even further, climbing to the summit of Long's Peak—an elevation of over 14,000 feet. The ascent and descent spanned two days, demanding grit, stamina, and no small amount of courage.[46]

Joining the group for part of the journey was Margaret Roebling, a teacher at Omaha High School of Commerce and a member of the club. Known as a "feminine Daniel Boone," Roebling was one of only three licensed female guides in Rocky Mountain National Park at the time. Her presence added both expertise and inspiration, embodying the adventurous spirit that defined the club's earliest trailblazers.[104]

This trip wasn't just a hike—it was a declaration. The Omaha Walking Club had arrived in the mountains, ready to explore, endure, and embrace the wild beauty of the West.

1922 – Paddles & Logging Trails at Lake Vermilion, Minnesota:

In August 1922, the walking club traded Nebraska's prairies for Minnesota's pine-scented air, spending two weeks at Lake Vermillion under the guidance of Edwin Jewell. Traveling by train, the group arrived to find their cabins nestled deep in the forest—a quiet retreat surrounded by towering trees and glassy water.[105]

Each day unfolded with a steady rhythm: four to five miles of hiking along old logging trails, followed by afternoons of fishing, canoeing, and campfire camaraderie. The lake offered both serenity and surprise. On one particularly memorable day, Harriet Mueller, Margaret Flickinger, Leslie Williams, and Carl Nagy embarked on a canoe trip that turned unexpectedly thrilling when rough waters tested their teamwork and nerve. They returned wet but triumphant, their adventure quickly becoming part of club lore.[3]

The Lake Vermillion outing was a trip marked not just by miles walked, but by memories made—quiet mornings in the forest, laughter echoing across the water, and the kind of shared experience that lingered long after the train ride home.

1923 – Scenic Drives & Hospitality at Black Hills:

In July 1923, sixteen members of the walking club returned to the Black Hills for a two-week adventure that blended rustic exploration with gracious hospitality. Under the steady leadership of Edwin Jewell—who oversaw the club's western outings for the third consecutive year—the group experienced the region's natural wonders and cultural warmth in equal measure.

The trip began with an auto tour around Hot Springs, South Dakota, courtesy of the local Chamber of Commerce, which provided a white sixteen-passenger touring car for two full days. The drive wound through pine-covered hills and mineral springs, culminating in a picnic supper at the country club. As twilight settled in, a poet offered readings and club members joined in song, turning the evening into a celebration of both place and friendship.

The generosity continued when soldiers at the National Sanitarium hosted a band concert in honor of the club—a gesture that underscored the community's appreciation for its spirited visitors.

From there, the group explored Wind Cave, marveled at a herd of elk, and ventured into Custer State Park, where sweeping vistas and quiet trails offered moments of awe and reflection.

This Black Hills journey was more than a getaway—it was a testament to the club's growing reputation and the joy of shared experience. With music, poetry, and panoramic views, the 1923 trip stitched together adventure and fellowship in a way only the Omaha Walking Club could.[106]

"Black Hills, South Dakota" 1923 OWC photo

1923 - Trail Friends at Lake Vermilion:

In August 1923, Harriett Mueller led a group of walking club members on another memorable trip to Lake Vermillion in Minnesota—one that proved the trail could lead not just to scenic views, but to new friendships. Upon arrival at the depot, the group was warmly welcomed by the Municipal Hiking Club of St. Paul, who promptly took charge of their baggage and whisked them away on a sightseeing tour by automobile.

The hospitality didn't stop there. The St. Paul hikers treated their guests to dinner, followed by a spirited baseball game that blurred the line between competition and camaraderie. The day continued with a swim in the lake, a picnic lunch, and a campfire that stretched into the evening, complete with singing under the stars.

When it was time to depart, the St. Paul hosts escorted the Omaha group back to the train—closing the trip with the same generosity and warmth with which it began.[107]

1923 – Miles of Majesty in Glacier National Park:

In July 1923, five intrepid members of the Omaha Walking Club set out for Glacier National Park, trading Nebraska's plains for Montana's towering peaks and alpine lakes. Led by Bess Dumont, the group spent two weeks immersed in the park's rugged beauty, hiking an astonishing 205 miles. Each day brought new vistas, winding trails, and the kind of quiet awe that only the mountains can offer. It was a journey of endurance and wonder—proof that the club's spirit of adventure knew no bounds.[108]

1924 – High Trails in Rocky Mountain National Park:

Fresh off their Black Hills triumph, fifteen members of the walking club set their sights higher in the summer of 1924—returning west to explore the rugged beauty of Rocky Mountain National Park. Once again, Edwin Jewell led the expedition, guiding the group through alpine passes, glacial valleys, and shimmering lakes tucked above the timberline. It was a journey of elevation in every sense.

The trip was not only a physical feat but a symbolic one. During the outing, a pristine mountain lake was named Lake Jewell in honor of Edwin's leadership and enduring contributions. Ever modest, Jewell requested the lake be named for the club instead—but was informed that geographic features couldn't bear organizational names.[109] Still, the spirit of the club was honored nearby with the naming of the "Omaha Walking Club" trail, a fitting tribute to the group's growing legacy in the West.

"Lochvale" In the Heart of the Rockies
*1924 * OWC photo by S. N. Hodes*

Preparation for the trip was no small matter. According to the Omaha Evening Bee, each hiker was advised to pack a regular hiking suit, extra trousers, and a small knapsack; multiple sets of medium-weight underwear; well-broken-in hiking boots roomy enough for both cotton and wool stockings (hobnails optional); and a pair of light camp shoes. Nights in the mountains called for a warm sweater or mackinaw, and sudden showers made a raincoat essential. The list continued with a mix of practical and personal items: drinking cup, camera, film, boot oil, adhesive tape, gloves, safety matches, shoelaces, bandanna handkerchief—and, in a nod to comfort and civility—powder puff and toothbrush.[110]

This trip marked another milestone in the club's history. With every step, the members carved their presence into the landscape—leaving behind not just footprints, but a trail named in their honor.

1924 - Gypsy Trip to Big Woods of Wisconsin:

While one group of walking club members scaled alpine passes in Colorado, another set off in a different direction—toward the deep forested heart of Wisconsin's Big Woods country. Led by Norman Weston, this 1924 expedition embraced a spirit of playful adventure, with members dressing as gypsies to match the trip's wandering nature. Their route, traveled by automobile, stretched over 1,500 miles through the Mississippi Valley and along the St. Croix River.[111]

*Gypsy trip in 1924 * STANDING: Homer Pennock, Emma Kment, Bess Turynek, Eva Begley, Jennie Sharkey, Martha Hoehne, Irene Higbee, SITTING: Norman Weston, Lyman Williams, Charles Gadway, Carl Nagy*

The journey was as immersive as it was scenic. The group explored hardwood groves, slept in tents or under open skies, and cooked most of their own meals over campfires. One of the trip's most memorable moments came during a visit to an Indian reservation, where members attended a powwow—an experience that added cultural depth to their forest immersion.

This wasn't a hike in the traditional sense—it was a roaming celebration of curiosity, camaraderie, and the open road. With costumes, campfires, and countless miles behind them, the travelers returned with stories that added a new kind of color to the club's growing legacy.[3]

1925 – Geysers & Trails on Trip to Yellowstone:

By July 1925, the Omaha Walking Club was no stranger to mountain air. In its fifth consecutive year of western excursions, twenty-seven members set out for Yellowstone National Park—ready for ten days of hiking, discovery, and camaraderie. Traveling from camp to camp by park buses, the group explored geyser basins, forested trails, and the surreal beauty of Yellowstone's volcanic landscape.[112]

"Yellowstone Outing Party"
*1925 * OWC photo by T. B. Murray*

One day was set aside for fishing, offering a quiet pause amid the adventure. Lines were cast, stories swapped, and the rhythm of the river replaced the crunch of boots on the trail. After their time in the park, the group continued west to Salt Lake City, adding a touch of urban exploration to their wilderness journey.[112]

This trip marked another milestone in the club's growing legacy of mountain travel—proof that their boots were made

"Fishing in Yellowstone Lake"
*1925 * OWC photo by E. S. Jewell*

for more than Nebraska trails. It was a journey stitched together by geysers, campfires, and the shared enjoyment of the open road.

1926 – Trails, Tents, & Trousers at Big Horn Mountains:

In July 1926, thirty-six members of the club boarded a sleeper train at Union Depot, bound for the wilds of Wyoming. Their destination: Piney Vale Lodge at the foot of the Big Horn Mountains. From the station in Sheridan, they traveled by automobile to the lodge, where their eleven-day, 125-mile pack horse hike would begin.[113]

The journey was a rhythmic blend of horseback riding and hiking—one hour in the saddle followed by two on foot. The terrain was rugged and the scenery breathtaking. An excerpt from the Omaha Daily News, published August 15, 1926, captured the spirit of the trip with colorful flair:

> …If you hear some pretty Omaha girl roll off choice "cuss" words, you can bank on it that she was probably a walking club hiker! Before leaving camp August 1 several of them vowed it would take a month to forget the words unconsciously picked up from Barney Smith, only guide along the Solitude trail through the Big Horn range around Cloud peak. Smith, rangy, blond of mustache and rough in appearance, has the reputation of being the most picturesque swearer in the Big Horn.
>
> Fingers burned on a hot griddle next winter may provoke a stream of cuss words, not offensive, but artistic, gathered from Barney…
>
> Wonderful things happened in that great outdoors.
>
> Presumably staid school marms didn't mind a whit when they wore trousers to dances where other girls wore sport dresses or silks – nope, indeed not. They gloried in their bifurcated garments.
>
> "Pop" Jewell, known in Omaha as Edwin S. Jewell, learned how to dance the fox trot there. The girls made him do it. They kidnapped him and took him to a dance at Story. There they tagged him with the announcement, "He's ours!" It took five girls to do it – but "Pop" danced every dance.

The adventure wasn't all dancing and colorful language. Six members—three women and three men—scaled Cloud Peak, standing 13,165 feet above sea level. Nights in the mountains were frigid, with each hiker bundled in four thick woolen blankets, and some resorting to heated stones tucked under their bedding to keep their feet warm.

Meals were cooked in the open and kept simple: ham, bacon, potatoes, fish, biscuits, canned vegetables and fruit, and a generous helping of flapjacks. Under Edwin Jewell's steady leadership, the trip blended grit, laughter, and mountain majesty—proving once again that the Omaha Walking Club knew how to turn a hike into a legend.[114]

*"Omaha Walking Club" at Burlington Station leaving for Big Horn Country in 1926 * From the KMTV/Bostwick-Frohardt Photo Collection, permanently housed at The Durham Museum*

A Legacy of Vacation Outings:

In addition to the trips made earlier in the 1920's, known club trips were made to:[73]

- 1927 – Black Hills in South Dakota
- 1928 – Medicine Bow National Forest in Wyoming
- 1929 – Superior National Forest in Minnesota
- 1930 – San Isabel National Forest in Colorado

- 1931 – Stapps Lake region in Colorado
- 1932 – Ross Teal Lake Lodge in northern Wisconsin
- 1932 – Big Horn Mountains

1928 *"Vacation Outing Party at Brooklyn Lodge—Medicine Bow National Forest, Wyoming" * OWC photo by Irene M. Higbee*

Mid-century brought renewed energy and expanded horizons:[73]

- 1950 – Stapps Lake region in Colorado
- 1954 – Estes Park in Colorado
- 1958 – Rocky Mountains in Colorado

One of the most memorable outings came in 1969, when thirty-four members boarded a chartered bus for a ten-day hiking trip in the Grand Teton Mountains—an epic celebration of the club's 50th anniversary.[1]

In the decades that followed, the tradition continued. From 1984 to 1994, vacation outings were mostly centered in Colorado, where alpine trails and mountain air remained a favorite backdrop for the club's enduring spirit.[1]

Whether hiking through pine forests, paddling across quiet lakes, or gathering around campfires in the shadow of mountain peaks, these trips reflected the club's core values: adventure, fellowship, and a deep appreciation for the natural world.

Weekend Escapes

Not every adventure required a long journey. Weekend trips to nearby camps and state parks became a beloved tradition for Omaha Walking Club members, offering a quick escape into nature without straying far from home. These outings—often just a short drive away—featured forest hikes, campfire meals, and quiet mornings by the lake. Whether exploring the trails of a State Park or going to a summer camp, members found joy in the simplicity of walking, relaxing, and reconnecting with familiar landscapes. These close-to-home excursions also kept the club's spirit alive between longer journeys.

In the 1920s, one favorite destination was Camp Iwaqua, a Camp Fire Girls' summer camp near Little Sioux, Iowa. Members traveled by bus, bringing their own bedding and a spirit of rustic adventure. These early getaways set the tone for decades of short-but-sweet excursions.[115]

The tradition continued with bus trips to Waubonsie Park near Sidney, Iowa—one in October 1938 and another in May 1940—where autumn leaves and spring blooms framed the club's hikes and picnics.[2] By 1950, car caravans replaced buses, and twenty-seven members spent Labor Day weekend at Lake Okoboji, enjoying three days of lakeside leisure.[116]

*Okoboji trip in 1950 * From the Omaha World-Herald/John Savage Photograph Collection at The Durham Museum*

Weekend outings remained a staple of club life through the mid-century and beyond.[1] Members gathered for Memorial and Labor Day weekends at places like Big Lake in Missouri (1954), Lake of Three Fires in Iowa (1954), and YMCA Camp Jefferson near Fairbury, Nebraska (1955). Spring Brook State Park hosted the club in 1957, while Ponca State Park became a favorite for both Memorial Day and Fourth of July celebrations in the 1960s. Gavins Point near Yankton, South Dakota offered a scenic escape in 1966.

In 1970, club members spent Memorial Weekend at the Ponderosa Ranch near Nebraska City. The following year, fifty members attended a lively Labor Day weekend at Riverview Vacation Ranch near Comstock, Nebraska, where the itinerary included hiking, wagon rides, swimming, volleyball, square dancing, and a moonlight hike.[117]

These weekend trips may not have involved mountain passes or sleeper trains, but they carried the same spirit of fellowship. Whether gathered around a campfire or strolling through a state park, members enjoyed the familiar landscapes just beyond their doorstep.

*Bus trip, ca. late 1940's * photo courtesy of Doug Wenger*

The Journey That Binds Us

Whether venturing to distant mountains or gathering at nearby parks, the Omaha Walking Club's travels have always been about more than the miles covered. These journeys—long and short—offered fresh air, shared stories, and a sense of belonging that stretched across generations. From train rides to car caravans, from alpine trails to wooded campsites, each trip added a new chapter to the club's legacy of exploration. No matter the destination, the heart of every journey was the same: walking together, discovering the world, and deepening the bonds that made the club a community.

Chapter 9:
Beyond the Trail: Games, Grit, and Good Fun

While hiking remained the heartbeat of the walking club, its pulse quickened with every canoe paddle, volleyball serve, and snow-packed sprint to the court. From lakeside swims to winter sledding, the club embraced a wide range of outdoor activities that kept members moving, laughing, and connected to nature in every season.

As member Doug Wenger recalled, the club's enthusiasm for sports extended well beyond hiking. His parents joined in the 1930s, and over the years, he witnessed firsthand the energy and devotion that defined the group. "There were many sports the Walking Club engaged in—tennis, horseshoes, ice skating, badminton, and softball among them," he wrote. "But the sport that really defined the Walking Club (besides walking of course) was volleyball." The court, tucked into a clearing east of the Shack, was rarely empty. Even in the dead of winter, members bundled up and stomped down snow just to play. Doug remembered returning home for Christmas and seeing clubbers head out in ten-degree weather—including his own mother, well into her seventies—ready to hit a frozen volleyball that, as he put it, felt "akin to hitting a bowling ball." It was tough, spirited, and unmistakably Omaha Walking Club.

The club's permanent camp buzzed with activity nearly every Sunday of the year. It began with simple games like "one old cat" and horseshoe pitching, then expanded to include canoeing, swimming, tennis, croquet, ping pong, and touch football. Seasonal favorites like skating parties and barn dances added flair to the calendar, proving that the club's love for movement was matched only by its love for fun.[2]

Whether hiking scenic trails or just plain loafing between matches, members enjoyed the recreation. These active pursuits weren't just pastimes—they were part of the club's enduring legacy of health, humor, and togetherness.

Up the Nets – Volleyball Takes Root

Decades before Nebraska earned its reputation as a volleyball powerhouse, the Omaha Walking Club was already stringing up nets and diving for serves in a forest clearing east of the Shack. The game arrived in the early 1920s, and word spread quickly. Its fast-paced rallies and quick breaks mirrored the endurance and agility honed on the trail—demanding teamwork, grit, and a dash of flair.[1]

By the 1930s, volleyball had become more than a pastime—it was a point of pride. The club began competing against other Omaha-area teams, stepping into the YMCA men's tournament in April 1935.[118] Though they entered with one win and three losses, they held their own until the Benson Blues defeated them and claimed the title.[119] The following year brought mixed results: the men of the Walking Club bested both the Blues and the Reds in early matches, only to fall again to Benson in a tight three-set showdown.[120]

*Volleyball in 1936 * photo courtesy of Doug Wenger*

The women of the Walking Club joined the fray as well. In January 1938, the club's women's team faced off against the YWCA girls in Council Bluffs, battling through five sets before conceding the match.[121] A few weeks later, they played Benson and again came up short.[122] By 1939, competition intensified. The South Recreation Center women's team defeated the club at the Jewish Community Center,[123] and later that month, both the men's and women's teams suffered losses in Florence.[124] December brought another round of tough matches, with the Benson men's team routing the club[125] and the Jewish Community Center women handing down a decisive defeat.[126]

Despite the scoreboard, volleyball remained a beloved tradition—played in all seasons and always with spirited determination. The club's early embrace of the sport laid the groundwork for decades of camaraderie and competition, proving that even off the trail, they knew how to rally.

Courtside Camaraderie: Tennis at the Shack

In 1924, the walking club added tennis to its list of activities by building a court near the Shack. Soon the soft "thwack" of ball on racquet became part of the weekend soundtrack. It was a fun mix of exercise, relaxation, and time spent together outdoors.[1]

*Tennis at the shack in 1935 * photo courtesy of Doug Wenger*

By 1937, the court was still in play, with some of the men performing maintenance by rolling its surface after a hearty pancake breakfast at the Shack—a ritual that blended sport, sustenance, and stewardship. But as interests shifted and other activities took center stage, the court was gradually left behind.[127] In 1945, it was officially abandoned, its lines fading into the forest floor.[1]

Though brief in its heyday, tennis added a graceful rhythm to the club's legacy—proof that even off the trail, members knew how to keep things moving.

Pickleball Pandemonium

In 2024, two of the members introduced the club to pickleball. What began on a weathered outdoor tennis court soon evolved into a favorite pastime among some of the walking club members. As summer heat intensified, the game moved indoors. Though pickleball was made an official club activity, games are usually unscheduled and played separately in metro area community centers where club members already have memberships. Despite having different locations for each group of players, pickleball became a spirited tradition, uniting members through shared laughter, friendly competition, and a love for movement.

Canoes, Kayaks, and River Crossings

With rivers and lakes never far from reach, the Omaha Walking Club found early joy in paddling as well as walking. Canoeing became a natural extension of their outdoor spirit—offering new ways to explore familiar landscapes and adding a splash of adventure to their hikes.

Canoeing on the Missouri in the early years
Photo courtesy of Doug Wenger

On October 1, 1922, members set out from Burlington Station in Council Bluffs for an all-day walk. After disembarking at Folsom, Iowa—a town that has since vanished—they hiked toward the Missouri River and crossed it by canoe, blending trail and water into one seamless journey.[128]

In October 1923, the club embarked on a 15-mile adventure that blended rail travel, river crossings, and campfire camaraderie. The day began with a train ride from Burlington Station to Plattsmouth, where members crossed the Missouri River by ferry. From there, they hiked north through the countryside, pausing for lunch around a campfire. Later in the day, a fleet of canoes awaited to carry them back across the river, allowing the group to complete their journey on foot all the way to the club's Shack. It was a full-circle outing—by train, by trail, and by water.[129]

Nearly a century later, in 2016, the club added kayaking to its repertoire. This summer alternative to hiking offered members a fresh perspective—gliding across quiet waters on an area lake. Whether by paddle or by foot, the club's love for movement and nature continued to flow forward, one ripple at a time.

Swimming Excursions

Swimming became a beloved part of the club's summer rhythm in the 1920s, with outings to Carter Lake, Lake Manawa in nearby Iowa, and the bustling Peony Park Pool. Members also took to the Big Muddy—the Missouri River—before it was fully channelized, turning riverbanks into impromptu beaches where laughter echoed over laps and splashes.[73]

One of the club's most legendary aquatic feats made headlines in 1925. Margaret Adams, Jim Baldwin, Walter Creel, and Esther Robinson swam twenty miles down the Missouri River, entering the water at Florence at 11 a.m. and emerging near the club's Shack at 6 p.m. Sustained by chocolate bars and chewing gum carried by Baldwin, the men admitted to being "dog tired" after their seven-hour journey—an unofficial event that became official lore.[130]

"Summer Sports at Shack"
*1924 * OWC photo by S. N. Hodes*

The club's reputation for boldness continued in 1930, when members Niels Pedersen, Douglas Van Valkenburgh, and Herman Weist broke through the ice on the Missouri River for a winter swim. The following week, joined by Esther Robinson, they tried again—but couldn't crack the frozen surface. With a strong wind and biting cold, they stood in swimsuits atop the ice while fellow members cheered from the shore. The practice, unsurprisingly, was short-lived and never adopted as an official activity.[131]

"Eager to Swim but the Missouri Ice was too Thick"
Omaha World-Herald, March 3, 1930

By the 1930s, the club introduced swimming guidelines: "Do not swim in river unless an expert swimmer" and "Do not wear bathing suits in the Shack." Sensible advice, given the club's growing numbers and increasingly adventurous spirit.[13]

Today, the tradition continues in gentler form. Each summer, members gather for swimming and a potluck at a private beach—an echo of earlier days, when water and fellowship flowed together.

Social Impact and Legacy

Over the years, the Omaha Walking Club embraced a wide range of outdoor activities—canoeing quiet streams and lakes, sledding down snowy slopes, swimming in local lakes, and field and court sports. While some of these pastimes have faded, today's members continue the tradition with favorites like swimming and pickleball. These current activities reflect the club's ongoing love for movement, camaraderie, and nature. And just as new generations once brought fresh ideas to the trails and rivers, future members will shape what comes next—ensuring the club's spirit of adventure endures in every step, paddle, and playful serve.

Chapter 10:
Club Canoes and River Tales

Not every journey began with boots on a trail—some started with paddles slicing through the Missouri's muddy current. In the early decades of the Omaha Walking Club, a spirit of adventure spilled off the land and into the water. Some of the members embarked on long-distance canoe trips, navigating bends and sandbars, camping under stars, and swapping stories beside riverside campfires. These weren't just outings—they were odysseys, stitched together by grit and the rhythm of the river.

Rafting the Big Muddy: A River Sport is Born

In the summer of 1923, a trio of walking club members—charter member David Broadwell, his brother Frank, and club caretaker Jim Baldwin—launched a new kind of adventure on the Missouri River. Using discarded railroad ties and scrap lumber scavenged from the Union Pacific yards, they built a sturdy raft and christened it with a tall pole flying a red bandana. A tripod at the center held inner tubes for safety, just in case the raft decided to come apart midstream.

From their launch point, the group would drift more than eight miles downriver to the club's Shack at Child's Point, a journey that took about two hours. At first, they tried steering with oversized paddles but quickly discovered they could maneuver better by jumping into the water and pushing the raft as they swam. In shallow stretches, they used poles to guide their floating platform. Along the way, they'd dive in for a swim, turning the trip into a moving celebration of summer.

*Jim Baldwin in the 1920s * photo by Bill Coons, courtesy of Fontenelle Forest*

They made five such voyages, building a new raft each time. Frank's wife and another woman joined two of the outings. At journey's end, the raft was either burned for firewood or sent further downstream—its purpose fulfilled.

This homemade sport, born of ingenuity and river grit, became a short-lived chapter in the club's legacy. It was equal parts engineering, endurance, and pure joy—proof that adventure didn't always require a mountain trail, just a few good friends and a river that knew how to carry them home.[132]

The Club's Women Join Jim on a Canoe Trip

In September 1925, walking club members Jim Baldwin, his sister Nell, and Isabel Zeigman set out on a two-day canoe journey that tested their endurance and deepened their bond with the river. They shipped a canoe to Blair and from there paddled approximately forty miles upstream along the Missouri River.

Jim steered from the stern while Nell and Isabel took turns in the bow, switching every two hours to keep pace and share the effort. The rhythm of paddles, the sweep of the riverbanks, and the quiet determination of the trio carried them through the journey. After reaching their turnaround point, they drifted back downstream toward the forest and the familiar trails near the club's Shack.

When they arrived, other club members were waiting to greet them—welcoming the paddlers home with admiration and likely a few questions about the river's moods. It was a trip marked by teamwork, stamina, and the kind of quiet adventure that defined the club's early years.[133]

Battling the Big Muddy: Raft Trip to Nebraska City

In September 1926, Walking Club members Jim Baldwin, David Broadwell, and Douglas Van Valkenburg took to the Missouri River on a raft once again—this time on a daring voyage from the Douglas Street bridge in Omaha all the way to Nebraska City. Their vessel was as rugged as the river itself: a crude raft built from telephone poles and driftwood, lashed together with determination and a healthy dose of improvisation.[134]

The journey was anything but smooth. Whirlpools and sandbars repeatedly snagged the raft, forcing the trio to wrestle their way free. A torrential rainstorm added to the drama, soaking the men as they pressed on wearing nothing but bathing suits. It was a test of endurance, grit, and good humor—hallmarks of the club's most memorable outings.[134]

Though the raft may have been temporary, the spirit of the trip was lasting. It was another chapter in the club's tradition of turning the Missouri River into a playground for invention, challenge, and camaraderie.

Peril on the River: Yankton to Omaha

In 1927, Walking Club members Jim Baldwin and David Broadwell undertook one of the most harrowing unofficial canoe trips in club history—a four-day, 400-mile journey down the Missouri River from Yankton, South Dakota to Omaha.

Jim Baldwin & Dave Broadwell
Omaha Morning Bee, July 4, 1927

The river was at flood stage the entire way, and as Baldwin later described it, "running wild."

Their canoe, battered by strong winds and unpredictable currents, faced extremes at every turn. In some stretches, the river spread out more than three miles wide with a sluggish flow; in others, it narrowed to a half-mile gorge where water surged with alarming speed. Above Sioux City, the river was devouring its banks—entire farms were collapsing into the current. Whitecaps broke over the sides of their canoe, forcing them to bail water for hours. At Sioux City, they finally hauled the canoe ashore to wait out the wind.

But the most terrifying moment came just ten miles north of Omaha, where they encountered a massive whirlpool—nearly a mile and a half in circumference. As they tried to cross it, the current flung them from Nebraska to Iowa and back again, spinning them in dizzying circles. At the center was a powerful "suckhold," a siphon-like force that pulled water down and hurled it back toward the edges in a boiling churn. For 45 minutes, Baldwin and Broadwell paddled with everything they had, fighting to escape the vortex. Eventually, they found a break in the current and shot through to safety.

By the time they landed at Douglas Street in Omaha, they arrived barefoot and shirtless due to a capsized canoe—weathered but triumphant. The journey was a testament to their grit and daring, and it made the newspapers for good reason. It was not just a canoe trip—it was a battle with the river itself.[135]

"That Keen Adventure"

In April 1930, two members of the club, Esther Robinson and Nell Baldwin, embarked on a canoe journey down the Missouri River to Kansas City. Esther

Robinson, who was a physical education instructor, later documented their experience in an account entitled "That Keen Adventure."

"In a canoe? You're crazy!"
"My dear—two girls? Do you have weapons with you?"
"You'll surely have a motor and sleep in a hotel at night——."

Such were the anything but encouraging remarks directed to us when we told friends of our plan to travel on the Missouri by canoe from Omaha to Kansas City. But in spite of their forebodings and the possibility of much rain in the middle of April we shoved off in our 17-foot canoe from the Omaha Walking club landing at 9 a. m. April 12 bound for Kansas City.

*Preparing the Canoe * Omaha World-Herald, June 1, 1930*

The desire to make such a trip had started a year ago when Nell Baldwin and I hitch-hiked to Kansas City and back. We looked at the river at St. Joseph and Kansas City and thought how much more interesting it would be in a canoe on the river than in an automobile on the highway.

We had paddled from Sioux City to Omaha accompanied by another girl, both of us had been swimming in the river for many years and with reasonably good weather we thought the trip would be very enjoyable.

We did not seriously consider the undertaking until a month before our departure. Then we spent many hours repairing and painting a canoe loaned us by a boating enthusiast of the Omaha Walking Club. James Baldwin, Nell's brother, who has taken many trips on the river, helped us get the boat in shape, and gave us pointers about paddling and the river.

Carrying Supplies * Omaha Sunday Bee News, April 13, 1930

Our equipment consisted of a tent, 10 blankets, a comforter, two shelter halves, slickers, two canvas water bags and four canteens; three paddles, flashlights, food, clothing, including a leather jacket, an army coat and a corduroy coat, frying pans, kettles, a coffee pot, toilet articles, two kodaks, cough drops, a hot water bottle and a dictionary. We lost only a frying pan lid during our six days on the water.

Canoeing on the Missouri is not a matter of drifting with the current as some people seem to think. One must be constantly on the alert for sand bars, snags, the direction of the wind and waves and the course of the river ahead. We encountered all of them the first day out. Above Plattsmouth the river makes a sharp bend north, the south shore is lined with stones and rip-rap of cut willows, the current throws itself against this bulwark and is just as suddenly diverted in the opposite direction. The rocks here are so large and extend so far out in the river bed that the waves are very choppy.

We hoped to make Nebraska City the first day. There was a little wind all day but not enough to make the water very rough. During a long afternoon stretch paddling was easy, the river calm and very wide ahead. Suddenly a terrific west wind hit us broadside. The waves became higher at once, first one and then another dashed over the bow of the boat, others came over the gunwales farther astern.

The current was very swift, the river stretched away a mile on either side and the boat was headed straight for a cut bank and snags. There was nothing to do but paddle hard and try to swing the boat so as to quarter the waves. As it was, we were getting them broadside, with a sideways heave that almost made us seasick. In five minutes, we were at the cut bank. The "shore" was 10 feet above our heads. We managed to turn the boat enough to avoid hitting the bank head-on, stepped out on a mound of dirt and tree roots, where we threw ourselves flat on our stomachs, hung on to the tie rope of the canoe, and let it ride the waves below us.

After chopping off an overhanging tree we lined the boat upstream a few yards, tossed blankets, frying pans, paddles and the rest of our equipment to the top of the bank. Clambering atop ourselves, we discovered snake grass as high as our waists and so thick that we could hardly make our way through it. Also a deserted log cabin, in which, under the best-looking part of the tar paper roof, we made our bed of 10 blankets, comforter, two coats, slickers, shelter halves, and all our heavy clothing.

Our campfire-cooked supper over, we attempted to crawl into bed. But the covering on top of us was so heavy we couldn't even get in. We had wanted to carry enough bedding with us so we could sleep comfortably with enough both under and over us. We certainly had it. After rearranging the bed, digging a ditch at the end of it, and setting pans to catch the worst drainage from the roof, we snuggled down to rest, dog tired, but happy over the experiences of our first day.

*Transporting the Canoe * Omaha World-Herald, June 1, 1930*

Sunday was a day of long, straight stretches of river. At Nebraska City we were told that we had had our bad water at the same place the boat of the Nebraska City men had capsized and the men drowned. This wasn't particularly cheering news. We were glad it was after our experience and not before.

There were more pleasure boats on the water at this town than any other we passed on the trip. Speed boats, outboard motors, and launches kept up a continual brr-r-r. Men on shore were cleaning their motors and repairing boats. All day we passed people in boats and on shore who were looking for the bodies of the drowned men. A large reward is offered for the recovery of each body.

Below the town, below the bridges, just river and more river. We were told that the next town was Brownville. We paddled for what seemed like many hours but no sign of a town appeared. All the time we heard and saw motorboats.

Esther and Nell * Omaha Evening Bee News, April 12, 1930

Sighted an airplane. Later we saw the airplane again. And what? The pilot circled low, waved to us, circled again, coming still lower—we could see him very distinctly as he leaned over the edge of the cockpit. When he was over the boat, plop! Something fell in the water, not 10 feet ahead of us. We quickly picked it up—a newspaper from home, with a letter from the pilot pasted on the outside. What a thrill! Air mail delivered to us in the middle of the Missouri river!

We learned later that Axel R. Swanson of Universal Air Lines, carrying mail on the Omaha, Kansas City and St. Louis route, was the pilot who delivered the Sunday paper so unexpectedly.

The airplane episode took place within sight of Brownville. The entire population congregated on the shore. We wrote cards and gave them to a man on shore to mail for us.

Downstream again! Wide river—no wind. We pitched camp that night among young willows. Before turning in I looked out between the tent flaps. Stars shining overhead, water gurgling softly below, unguentine on the sunburn—ready for a long night's rest.

More than one morning we were glad we had put dry wood under the overturned canoe. Dense fog surrounded us one morning, two other times we had to lie in bed late and wait for the rain to stop.

We lost our complexions but not our appetites. Our menu was varied: eggs, bacon, coffee, flapjacks, stewed apricots and rhubarb for breakfast; bread and butter, apple butter, peanut butter, cheese, cookies, oranges, marmalade and crackers for lunch; and potatoes, spaghetti, to-matoes, salmon wiggle (a dish consisting of salmon, hard boiled eggs, pimentos, peas and cream sauce) and beans for supper. Variations and combinations of these supplies made delicious meals.

Below the ferry at Nemaha the river is very narrow. We encountered high waves and shipped quite a little water. The wind blew incessantly all of our third day on the river.

Tuesday morning we passed Rulo, Kans. Here the ferries, Little Joe and Rulo Belle, were tied up, also a comfortable appearing houseboat painted green.

Scenery along the Missouri is constantly changing. Yellow-green cot-tonwood trees and willows are found for miles along the banks in every conceivable grouping and stage of growth. There are also many stretches of towering rock-bound bluffs covered with dark green hard-wood trees with flowering red buds scattered everywhere. We saw cardi-nals, swallows, kingfishers and yellow flickers in the woods, and gulls, blue herons, cranes and thousands of geese on the river.

At 4:30 in the afternoon we began to look for a good camping place. Tuesday at that time a storm was coming up, the likeliest-looking camp site was atop a 15-foot bank. A tent was already pitched there but the shore ahead looked unpromising. We decided to go to the trouble of lug-ging our camping stuff to the top of the bank rather than paddle on.

Two fishermen, occupants of the other tent, helped us pitch ours and gave us coal oil to start our fire. They were William Walker and Mr. Zecker of Nodaway, Mo., a mile up the shore. They had lived in their tent all winter. How they withstood the cold we couldn't figure out as they had only an oil stove and little bedding. They fish for a living,

*Kansas City or Bust * Omaha Sunday Bee News, April 13, 1930*

selling their catch to people in nearby towns and occasionally to St. Joseph markets.

Our tent looked like it was put up on the bias. One side was stretched tight and the other side sagged, the front pole leaned to the southward and the flaps toward the north. But it stayed up and kept out the rain.

We arrived at St. Joseph at noon Wednesday. I went uptown to buy unguentine and kodak films while Nell stayed with the boat.

Below St. Joseph the government is working on the river to make it navigable. Break waters of piles project out from the shore, and cut banks are being sloped off and lined with riprap of interlaced willows and stonework.

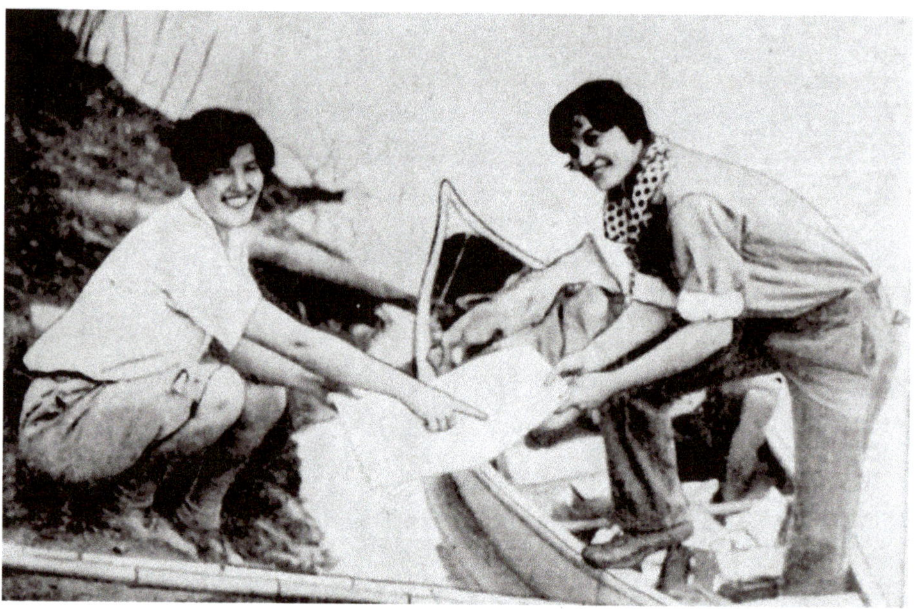

*Esther and Nell * Omaha World-Herald, June 1, 1930*

Huge paddle-wheelers, steamboats, launches, freight barges, and tugs make a hum of activity wherever the crews are at work. Construction companies from St. Louis, Kansas City, and Lincoln, Neb. are employing hundreds of men. Pile drivers ker-chug driving the logs into the mud and sand. Sawmills cut cotton wood trees into planks. Hammers ring as men lay the decks of the new barges. Dynamite blasts stumps from the clearings. In Omaha one reads about the appropriations made by congress for river work, but at St. Joseph and below the work is actually progressing.

Thursday—what a day that turned out to be. We started with wind and had it all day. During a half hour of particularly rough water the bow of the boat repeatedly dipped into the waves ahead. Water slushed in the bottom from bow to stern and back. The boat was headed almost into the wind, and the current was very swift. We traveled fast but a good deal of it was up and down.

After a long pull we reached Atchison. We were cold, wet, and hungry, but decided to paddle farther before stopping as we wanted to reach Leavenworth that night. Only on this day did we need all the clothing we brought with us. I had on a shirt, sweater, flannel middie, and leather jacket with the army overcoat and a slicker wrapped around my legs. Nell was as bulkily attired in two pairs of pants, two shirts, a sweater, and the corduroy coat.

Just above Leavenworth we saw the worst water the Missouri has in any part of it we have been on. The river flows south, makes a sharp turn, and less than half a mile downstream is flowing directly north. The waves looked like ocean breakers only more uneven.

We pushed and pulled our way along the rocky shore, trying to keep out of the monstrous waves and yet not hit the rocks. We hugged a sand bar on the inside of a bridge pier. Further downstream the water was a little better.

The last morning of the trip we gave our surplus food to Jimmy Gerski, a fisherman from near Leavenworth. He stopped running his lines long enough to help us load our boat.

Bright sunshine on the last day made us regret leaving the river in spite of the memory of our one cold day. As it had rained only at night we had been able to keep all of our blankets and other equipment dry.

We sighted Kansas City a long way off. The tall buildings and smoke hovering over a town are easily distinguishable hours before you get near them.

Smells and noise, bridges, trains, bums, dumps, and dirt go with a city. It was unpleasant after the fresh wind on the river. We docked beside a sand barge at the municipal wharf. An obliging warehouse watchman helped us unload and arrange our boat and outfit for shipment home.

A canoe trip is not easy. It really means hard work most of the time. But the sun and water, the joy of paddling on around the bend, of going down the old river in spite of what she puts in your way, are returns worthy of the effort.

This journey down the Missouri River was more than a test of stamina—it was a celebration of friendship, curiosity, and bold spirit. Esther's vivid storytelling preserved not just the details of the trip, but the joy of venturing into the unknown with a paddle, a plan, and a trusted companion.[52]

Six Weeks on the Water: Great Falls to Omaha

In July 1930, club member Herman Weist came up with an idea for an ambitious canoe journey. The plan was bold: paddle the Missouri River from Great Falls, Montana all the way to Omaha. Jim Baldwin agreed to go with him. With their 18-foot canoe stowed in the baggage car, they traveled by train to their launch point, where the river's upper reaches greeted them with treacherous rapids and unpredictable currents.[136]

Jim Baldwin
World-Herald, July 1930

The journey spanned 1,700 miles and took roughly six weeks to complete. Along the way, they navigated hazards, endured fatigue, and witnessed the shifting moods of the river—from wild and narrow gorges to wide, slow-moving stretches. It was a test of endurance and teamwork, and a testament to their adventurous spirit.[137]

Canoe, Camp, Repeat

For the club members who took to the water, the Missouri River offered a different kind of trail—one that flowed, meandered, and demanded a new rhythm. Paddle by paddle, mile by mile, they carved out stories that didn't need official agendas or printed notices. Just a canoe, a campfire, and the kind of companionship that turns effort into joy.

Chapter 11:
Connecting Through Community

From the beginning, the Omaha Walking Club was never just about the miles—it was about the people met along the way. As the club grew, so did its connections beyond its own circle. Members found joy not only in walking together but in joining forces with other groups, sharing stories, laughter, and a common purpose. Whether hosting, volunteering, or simply showing up to hike with another club, the Omaha walkers brought their signature spirit of camaraderie wherever they went.

Campfires and Connections

From its earliest years, the Omaha Walking Club understood that walking could do more than strengthen legs—it could strengthen relationships. Whether hosting nature lovers, civic groups, or fellow hiking clubs, the club built a reputation for warm hospitality, shared trail wisdom, and a knack for turning a simple outing into a meaningful connection.

In May 1921, the club joined forces with the Nebraska Audubon Society and the Nebraska Ornithological Union during a joint conference in Omaha.[138] The following day, club members led field exercises in Fontenelle Forest alongside public school teachers and students, blending education with exploration.[139] The following year, in March 1922, the club hosted a recital of readings and music at the YMCA, showing that its interests extended beyond the trail.[140]

That same month, the O.F.F. Club of St. Agnes Parish hiked from their church through Mandan Park, descending the steep bluff to the riverbank east of Camp Gifford. The Omaha Walking Club welcomed them with open arms—and open flames—offering use of their grounds and preparing coffee and wieners over a campfire. It was one of many moments where the Shack became a social crossroads.[141]

Throughout the 1920s and '30s, the club extended invitations to university students, businesswomen, youth organizations, and nature clubs.[142] In October 1922, students and faculty from the University were invited to join a Sunday hike through the Florence area, led by Irene Tauchen.[143] In 1923, members were welcomed by the Municipal Hiking Club of St. Paul, Minnesota,[107] and that same year, the club joined the Associated Mountaineering Clubs of America, signaling its growing national presence.[1]

In April 1928, members of the Eureka Club—an active organization within the Social Settlement—participated in a moonlight hike to the Omaha Walking Club Shack.[144] On July 4, 1930, the volleyball team from the Y traveled to the Shack to compete against the Walking Club team.[13]

From 1931 to 1939, the club exchanged annual visits with the Hastings Outdoor Club, including joint outings in Crete in 1939 and 1940. Edwin Jewell was instrumental in forming this club.[145] They also hosted and visited clubs from Sioux City[146] and Lincoln, forming a regional network of trail-minded friends.[2] In 1935, they welcomed Grace Ficken of the Georgia Appalachian Trails Club for a luncheon at Omaha's Aquila Court tearoom, where she spoke about trails in the eastern U.S.—a rare and treasured exchange of hiking cultures.[147]

The club's Shack became a hub for social gatherings and educational outings. In 1926 and 1931,[148] members of the Omaha Business and Professional Women's Club were guests at the Shack, footsore but delighted.[149] Later that year, the two clubs traveled together to Nebraska City to visit Arbor Lodge.[150] Over the next decade, the Shack hosted groups ranging from the Technical High School Junior Girl Reserves (who made taffy apples over a campfire)[151] to the Knights of Columbus slenderizing class, who hiked in for fresh air and fellowship.[152]

"Dinner under the trees at the shack with six visitors from the Hastings Walking Club as guests of the OWC" Oct. 4, 1931 * OWC photo by R. L. Andrews

Nature clubs, athletic associations, and church groups all found common ground—literally—at the Shack. The Women's Athletic Association,[153] the German Club of the University of Omaha,[73] the Jewish Community Center women's physical education class,[154] the Omaha Methodist League of Youth,[155] and the Brown Park Club[156] all made the trek. In 1938, the club traveled by bus to Lincoln for a sports field day with the Lincoln Outdoor Club, enjoying baseball, tennis, and volleyball at Pioneer Park.[157]

Even national events found echoes in the forest. In May 1940, more than 40 members from the Omaha Nature Study Club, Fontenelle Forest Association, and the Girl Scouts joined the walking club for a joint hike and picnic. A newspaper article noted the peaceful sounds of nature as a stark contrast to the war unfolding in Europe—a poignant reminder of the refuge the forest offered.[158]

The club's hospitality continued into the 1940s and beyond. In 1941, they entertained 39 traveling members of the Minneapolis Municipal Hiking Club with a full day of sports, hiking, dinner, singing, and dancing.[159] In 1947, they led the Hanscom Park Garden Club on a wildflower walk through Fontenelle Forest.[160] In 1949, they hosted members of the Mississippi Trails Club[161] and the Fontenelle Forest Association, discussing bird migration and forest conservation over dinner.[162]

Even the Omaha Camera Club became regular companions, joining hikes and capturing the club's spirit in snapshots.[163] In 1970, the Couple's Club of St. Luke's Lutheran Church enjoyed a nature walk followed by a chicken dinner at the Shack.[164] And in 1989, the club hiked with the Trailblazers, continuing a legacy of shared steps and shared stories.[1]

Through it all, the Omaha Walking Club proved that networking doesn't require name tags or conference halls—just a good trail, a warm fire, and sensible footwear.

Clubhouse, Meet Cockpit

In February 1929, the quiet trails near the Omaha Walking Club's shack became the unlikely stage for a high-flying drama. Jack Knight,[20] a daring airmail pilot who had been a flight instructor during WWI—and later celebrated for his role in the first overnight transcontinental airmail relay—was battling a fierce snowstorm as he flew low over the Nebraska landscape, trying to get his bearings.[165] He had missed Fort Crook, his intended destination, and was now skimming the treetops over the forest near the Shack.

*Jack Knight * San Diego Air and Space Museum Archive photo*

The swirling snow clogged his engine, causing it to sputter and stall—leaving Knight with no choice but to make an emergency landing. Bill Coons, his wife Inez, and Charles Gadway[166] witnessed the descent with a mix of awe and alarm. They waved their arms frantically to direct the pilot to a clearing near the Shack.

With trees looming ahead and low visibility, he managed to thread the needle and touch down just shy of disaster. Rushing to assist, they helped Knight and his passenger—a sharply dressed salesman from New York City—out of the snow-covered aircraft.

The salesman, clad in low-cut shoes and a city-slicker suit, looked wildly out of place in the wintry Nebraska woods. While Knight took the incident in stride, the salesman was less enthused. When Knight prepared to take off again the following day, the salesman politely declined to reboard, opting instead for the far less adventurous route: the train.[21]

The clubhouse buzzed with stories of the landing for weeks. For the walkers who saw it firsthand, it was a reminder that even the skies could deliver unexpected guests—and that sometimes, the trail leads straight to history.

Where Footsteps Meet Purpose

The Omaha Walking Club didn't just walk through nature—they rolled up their sleeves to protect it. From tree planting to firefighting, their volunteer efforts formed a quiet but powerful legacy of stewardship, often carried out with little fanfare and a lot of heart.

One of the club's earliest neighbors was Boy Scout Camp Gifford. In April 1922, Judge Charles Foster and fellow club members joined the Scouts to plant fifty trees around the camp—a gesture that rooted the club's conservation ethic early on.[1] Just months later, in August 1922, twenty members—mostly men— tackled the grueling task of rip-rapping the banks of the Missouri River at Child's Point peninsula. Using wood from the forest and securing it with cables, they worked to prevent erosion. Many spent the night at the Shack to rise early and continue the labor the next morning.[167] A decade later, the club returned to reinforce the same stretch of riverbank.[168]

Tree planting remained a recurring theme, with saplings added throughout the years. In 1949, members gathered bushels of acorns and walnuts to send to Scottsbluff, where the Lions Club used them for planting efforts—an act of ecological sharing that stretched across the state.[169]

The club's Conservation Committee took a proactive role in education and preservation. One year they placed 200 cardboard signs across Fontenelle Reserve, Mandan Park, and Rainbow Point, urging visitors to protect birds, wildflowers, and trees.[3] During the years when Fontenelle Forest operated on donations rather than formal memberships, the club helped promote support through the Friends of Fontenelle Forest initiative.[22]

From 1930 to 1960, Fontenelle Forest operated on a limited budget, with Omaha Walking Club members assisting in trail upkeep and firefighting.[22] But perhaps the most dramatic volunteer efforts came in response to fire. In the hot, dry 1930s, multiple blazes scorched acres of forest. Club members, often alongside Boy Scouts, helped contain the flames.[22] To formalize their readiness for firefighting, the club created an Emergency Volunteers list in the late 1940s, which remained active for decades.[1]

After losing their second Shack to fire, the club faced another major blaze in 1953, which consumed 80 acres of heavy timber. The Bellevue Volunteer Fire Department, off-duty firemen from Offutt Air Force Base, and club members fought tirelessly to extinguish it—only to be saved, finally, by a wet snowfall.[170]

In April 1956, a fire threatened Fontenelle Forest and nearby railroad tracks, burning over 300 acres. With no water supply and few roads, traditional firefighting crews couldn't reach the area. Members of the Walking Club and Chicago, Burlington & Quincy Railroad section crews stepped in, stopping the blaze through teamwork.[171]

In May 1966, a major fire in the forest was averted. A telephone relay mobilized 50 to 60 volunteers in minutes. Offutt volunteer firemen, the Omaha Walking Club, and Fontenelle Forest Association were on this chain call. Thanks to this rapid response, a potentially devastating fire was contained with minimal damage.[172]

In more recent years, the club extended its service beyond the forest. In 1992, they joined the Adopt-A-Highway program, maintaining stretches of roadside with the same care they gave to trails and trees.[1]

Whether planting saplings, maintaining trails, or answering the call of a fire alarm, the Omaha Walking Club proved that walking was only part of the journey.

Helping Hands and Handshakes

Whether teaming up or socializing with outside organizations, lending a hand to a stranded pilot, or pitching in to support the community, the Omaha Walking Club has always been more than a collection of hikers—it's been a network of neighbors, helpers, and friends. These stories, from the extraordinary to the everyday, reflect the club's enduring spirit of connection and generosity. Through shared adventures and acts of service, the club has left footprints not just on trails, but in the hearts of those it's met along the way.

Chapter 12:
Trail Tales: Member Reflections

Every step taken with the Omaha Walking Club has left more than just footprints—it's left stories. These stories span generations, tracing footsteps through forest paths, clubhouse corners, and family lore. Whether remembered firsthand or retold from parents' adventures, each reflection offers a glimpse into the club's evolving spirit—its friendships, challenges, quiet romances, and the rhythms of life shaped by time and trail.

Raised by Trees (and Parents)

Shortly before the club's centennial, Tom Lazure shared some of his memories of spending time in Fontenelle Forest as a child. His grandfather Charles Sr., father Phil, three uncles and their wives all belonged to the Omaha Walking Club at one time or another. His uncle's wife Trudy is still a member. Tom grew up spending time at the clubhouse in Fontenelle Forest and took part in many Sunday walks. He wrote in the Bulletin:

> Most of my memories are going down to Fontenelle Forest. We'd meet at what at the time was called the Donut Shack – basically a parking lot with a small building and the beginning trail heads.
>
> The night hikes were a lot of fun! From the Donut Shack, down along the Missouri, we'd go back into the deep dark woods and finally to "The Shack." The Shack was home base to us kids and typically it was a race to get down there if there were other kids involved. We were a pretty competitive bunch!
>
> What was so surprising is that even at a young age, in the darkness of the night, no flashlights, our parents trusted us enough to take to the trail and be out of sight of the group with no problem. Some, at least today, would be arrested for child abuse. But they knew we knew the trail and were smart enough that if we got confused we'd back track or yell out for help. And that never happened.
>
> We'd get down there ahead of the rest and wait for someone to show up with the key to the Shack. The overnights demanded that everyone that

could get their mattresses from a storage area and get their sleeping stuff set up. There were two shelters for sleeping, one for the guys and one for the ladies. They were screened in to keep the bugs out and at times it may get a little cold. When that happened you could always go into the Shack where the fireplace would be going and it'd be toasty warm! I would be remiss if I didn't mention it got a little scary waking up having to use the outhouse which was about, what seemed like a ½ block away.

During the daytime, there was always something to do. The Shack always had a number of games inside, but outside was more to our liking. There was a volleyball court, horseshoes, hikes to the river, wood collecting for the fireplace, frisbee, and occasionally us kids would go over to the only farmhouse around and ride horses with them. Then at night we'd tell scary stories around the outside campfire, roast marshmallows and take another night-time hike.

One time I remember just a few of us kids headed back down toward the river. The moon was fairly bright and you could hear every little noise from the crickets to an owl hooting. As we got to some of the farm fields you could see and I'm not exaggerating, probably 40-75 deer out feeding. As we got past the excitement of the numbers we moved on. We went about another; I'd say 3-4 blocks and my good friend Greg thought he saw a mountain lion in a nearby tree. By the time I could ask him if he really saw something, he and my older brother Phil were already heading back at a dead sprint! It didn't take long for me to catch up and we all made it back safely; huffing, puffing, and laughing all at the same time. Of course, as the story gets retold it gets better and better as time goes on. Don't know what Greg actually saw and I'm not calling him a liar. It's dark, you can't see 5 feet in front of you and who wants to stick around to find out if it was or not!

Club member Doug Wenger also grew up spending time with the Omaha Walking Club. He gave a speech and shared photos at the centennial celebration in 2019. An excerpt from the transcript relates to his childhood:

My parents were both active in the club for most of their very long lives and our childhoods were filled with club activities and club members. It was a great way to grow up. We spent countless summer weekends on Saturday overnights at the Shack waking up Sunday morning to the sound of the forest birds.

Where Romance Met Trail Dust

Doug's parents, Ken and Doris Wenger, met in the Omaha Walking Club in the 1930s and later married. He spoke about the club's romances in his speech:

> After only a little more than 10 years of existence, one of the OWC bulletins mentioned that dozens of marriages had already resulted between couples who first met at the club. Most people don't realize that the Omaha Walking Club was an early precursor to and probably even more successful than today's dating sites – like Match.com. The reasons aren't hard to decipher. They spent their days participating in hikes, sports, and other activities surrounded by nature's beauty, then an evening of talk, laughter, and singing around a fireplace with its dancing flames and glowing embers. And when the fire had died, they walked two miles back to their cars at the Donut House through the dark woods illuminated by moonlight. That makes a very powerful combination.

> Here's an example of how powerful this combination was and what it could overcome. Henry Mollner was a single club member in 1933 when he read this poem to Margaret Otto, another single, in front of the gathered members. Henry's poem covered the many ways he had improved himself under Margaret's constant pointers. Among Henry's lines were:

> *And I'm the luckiest of boys*
> *To hear her sermons face to face.*

> Then in Henry's conclusion he said:

> *Now Margaret I realize that I've improved*
> *A hundredfold since I met you*
> *....*
> *But now, since each unmanly trait*
> *Is parked forever on the shelf,*
> *I really think it would be great*
> *If you'd improve a bit, yourself.*

> Now I have no idea if Margaret ever improved – even a bit - but apparently Henry had improved enough already! They were married soon after and had six children.

Doug also shared memories of his parents' courtship:

> They met at a Walking Club Halloween party in 1936—Mom was walking along the trail to the Shack with a girlfriend when Dad jumped out from behind a tree dressed as the Devil. Mom was not impressed. Apparently her impressions changed because they got married 4 years later.

Ken & Doris Wenger in 1940
Photo courtesy of Doug Wenger

> The relationship between my parents and the Omaha Walking Club turned out to be a match made in heaven. My Dad was an avid walker all his life. In the 1930's he was also an AAU All-American volleyball player. And my Mother's senior South High School yearbook entry (before she had even heard of the Walking Club) listed her two main outside interests as—hiking and volleyball! So, it's easy to see why they were so attracted to the Club and to each other.

Stories from the WWII Years

Doug shared some of his dad's stories of the club in the WWII era in his speech too:[13]

> The Second World War had a dramatic impact on the OWC. About 28 members, both male and female, joined the services or one of the aid organizations and were gone from Omaha during that time. That's about one-fourth of the club membership then. To keep up with their assignments, the bi-monthly OWC Bulletin originally started with a column called "Doughboy Dope" where the latest news on Club members serving was noted. But while the column continued, the name was quickly changed. It seems the Doughboys from the Army didn't appreciate the word "Dope" being associated with them. And those members in the other services weren't too keen on being called Doughboys either. So,

the column became the Bugle Blast for the duration of the war and after
- until everyone had returned home.

Our Dad and several others joined the Army. Hoke Smith was servicing
planes in Europe for the Army Air Corps. Pete Marchetti was an officer
in the Coast Guard serving in the South Pacific. Ted Richling was a
lawyer for the Army Judge Advocate General Corp and spent a long
time on General George Patton's staff in Paris. Hoke Smith's wife
Grace was stationed in several cities around the country where she
would organize local USO organizations and got them up and running.
And some of the women were in the WAACS. Our mother kept her
own list for everyone out of town – which she called her Worry List.

The OWC kept the memberships of all who were serving during the war
active with no dues required. But with so many of the members gone,
money was even tighter than normal. Now the Club had always done a
variety of fundraisers to earn money for building and repairing the
Shack and other expenses – like bake sales, Pancake Breakfasts, Spaghetti Dinners, and Chicken Dinners which had always been one of the
favorites.

So, plans were made – by the women who were left including my Mom
- to hold a Chicken Dinner at the Shack. Although there were very few
men around, they did find one, a relatively new member named Don,
who said he had access and could bring the chicken.

The morning of the Chicken Dinner arrived and the women were busy
at the Shack getting everything prepared when Don showed up with the
chickens – 10 live ones! After some minutes of consternation and with
the arrival of the guests getting closer, the women decided they had
enough farm experience and mid-western determination among them to
handle the challenge. So, they proceeded with the beheading, plucking,
etc and the rest of the dinner went off without a hitch – along with many
comments about how fresh the chicken tasted.

An OWC bulletin at the end of the war celebrated the fact that all of the
active members of the Club who went off to war came back safely. But
that wasn't the complete story. There was a couple named Kit and
Doug Gehrman who had been members and active in the Club until
about 1937 when they moved to California. They had been among my
mother's best friends. Doug had enlisted in the Marines at the start of

the war. Unfortunately, during the seven-month campaign known as the Battle of Guadalcanal, Doug was among the 1,600 US troops who were killed in action. When I came along about 18 months later in August of 1944 at the German POW camp in Greeley, Colorado where my Dad was in charge of the guards, my parents named me after Doug in his honor.

Steps That Stayed With Us

And so, from forest flirtations to heroic chicken chases, these reflections prove that the Omaha Walking Club was never short on drama, charm, or culinary improvisation. Whether passed down through family lore or lived in muddy boots, each tale adds a stitch to the club's delightfully lopsided quilt of history. If memory serves—and sometimes it doesn't—there's always another story waiting just around the bend.

Chapter 13:
The Hermit of Fontenelle Forest

Jim Baldwin once walked in step with the community. As an early member of the Omaha Walking Club, he led group hikes, served as the club's lifeguard, shared stories, hosted parties and was caretaker of the clubhouse. He always loved the outdoors and living in a rustic shack, but over time, something shifted. He gradually withdrew from the club and society itself. Eventually, he made his home in a cave in Fontenelle Forest, embracing a life of quiet isolation. This chapter tells the story of Baldwin's final decades of life as a hermit, and the enduring legend he left behind in the ravines and shadows of Fontenelle Forest.

From Club to Cave: The Quiet Life of Jim Baldwin

Jim Baldwin didn't just live in Fontenelle Forest—he became part of its folklore. Several years after returning from World War I, he turned his back on city life and settled into the thickets near Bellevue in a shack with his father and brother.[36] Although they were farmers, Jim wasn't particularly interested in working hard at that or any kind of traditional job.[13] His father and brother eventually moved, but Jim stayed. What began as a solitary retreat evolved into a quiet life rich with reading, storytelling, and unexpected fame.

As Jim grew older, he became a colorful character. In the late 1940s, he let his beard grow wild, gradually taking on the look of a forest hermit. He relished the nickname of "hermit," and leaned into the persona with theatrical flair.[173] People would trek through the forest to

*Jim Baldwin's dwelling in the forest * photo by Bill Coons, courtesy of Fontenelle Forest*

see him. With glee, he entertained scouts and hikers with animated stories.[19] His shack on 43 acres of land was stocked with canned fruits and vegetables.[174]

Despite his reputation as a hermit, he wasn't anti-social. He was beloved by children, hikers, and members of the Omaha Walking Club, who recalled his warmth and sense of adventure.[175]

*In the 1950s, Walking Club member Doris Wenger led this group of Girl Scouts on a field trip to hear Hermit Jim's tall tales. Her daughters are in the front row. Barb (3rd from the left) and Judy (5th from the left) were part of the adventure—and both are still Walking Club members in 2025. * Photo courtesy of Doug Wenger*

Jim's life during his final years wasn't without hardship. He eventually moved from his shack to a cave. On June 13, 1959, two Boys Town residents—who had previously visited his cave and listened to his stories—attempted to rob him, leaving him beaten and blind in one eye. He spent over a month in the hospital. But when he returned—clean-shaven and smiling—the community rallied. Kids swarmed around him, and Jim danced for joy. "I could hear kids playing nearby and finally was able to get a glimpse of them through my window," he said. "I had a little trouble seeing them with my one remaining eye but it seems to be growing stronger."[175]

His welcome home was nothing short of cinematic. KMTV, the Bellevue Press, and Offutt Air Force Base coordinated a celebration. A black limousine chauffeured him from the Veterans Hospital, and a helicopter flew him closer to his cave than any car could reach. Mayor Vernon Woodle greeted him, and Jack Wells led a small band. Jim hugged the children and shared how lonely he'd been for their company.[175]

Since he was unable to tend his garden during his time in the hospital, many people donated canned goods to him. After returning home, Jim occasionally missed the hospital nurses and patients. The feeling was mutual—when Jim was discharged, the nurses and patients on his ward lined up to say goodbye.[175]

Club member Henry J. Mollner wrote in the Omaha World Herald several years later:

I first got to know Jim at the Omaha Walking Club in the mid-20's. Because of a disagreement with his boss, he quit his job and swore he never would work in any city again. He built a shack about two miles south of Camp Brewster overlooking the Missouri. A small garden and chickens he raised provided food. He would chop wood for the fireplace at the club and watch our clubhouse during the week to prevent vandalism. For this, he would be rewarded with a "Sunday meal," as he called it, every weekend.

Jim was an expert swimmer. It was a pleasure to swim down to a sand bar with him and listen to him spin yarns. He left the woods just once. In the '30s a club member, Herman Weist, persuaded him to take a canoe trip with him from Fort Benton back to Omaha.

Always friendly, Jim did much to make people happy. Many a lost group was guided back to right trails. In his last years youngsters made a game out of who could find the "hermit" first. He should have been the last person on earth to be beaten by hoodlums.[176]

In November 1960, students at Fort Crook School assembled Thanksgiving baskets for families in need as well as for Jim Baldwin. Each family received a 10-pound turkey in addition to canned and fresh foods. Jim Baldwin did not receive a turkey—not due to a lack of funds, but because he was a vegetarian.[177] For Christmas, the Bellevue American Legion Auxiliary sent Jim a Christmas box.[178]

That winter was exceptionally cold. Visitors discovered Baldwin with a frozen left leg, leading to a six-week stay at the Veteran's Hospital. Upon his release, he returned home and thanked the nurses and doctors for not cutting his beard.[179]

Not long after his release from the hospital, Jim Baldwin bid farewell to his woodland refuge and moved in with his sister Nell.[180] She still lived at the Baldwin family's longtime residence—a modest home at 127 Martha Street in Omaha near the Missouri River that Jim had also lived in decades earlier.[181]

The following appeared in the Public Pulse section of the Evening World-Herald on June 16, 1966 after Baldwin's death:[182]

The death of Jim Baldwin, "the Hermit of Fontenelle Forest," marked the passing of one of the most colorful persons I ever knew.

As a member of the Omaha Walking Club in the '20s and '30s I learned to know Jim as a warm friend, not only to our club members, but also to Boy Scouts, hikers and anyone who cared to listen to his stories.

Jim roamed the woods, guiding lost hikers to the right trails for home, kept a watchful eye on our Shack, to prevent vandalism. And a swim down the river to a "special" sand bar, to rest and spin yarns, was an experience I shall never forget.

-- HENRY J. MOLLNER

Jim Baldwin didn't just retreat from the world—he reimagined how to live in it. His cave may have been tucked away in the woods, but his stories, kindness, and eccentric charm reached far beyond the trees.

Chapter 14:
Carrying the Trail Forward

Over one hundred years of trails, shacks, ballfields, and campfire songs have intertwined to form a living tapestry—each thread dyed by laughter, sweat, song, or silence. From that first hike in 1919 to today, every gathering has layered new meaning onto the soil of Fontenelle Forest and the surrounding area. In tracing this arc, we discover how a simple walking club blossomed into a multi-dimensional community whose heartbeat still echoes in every footstep.

In 2019, weeks after the final clubhouse was destroyed by floodwaters, the club held a celebration of their first 100 years. Most of the traditions continued without the use of a clubhouse. The trails in the forest floodplain had been wiped out by months of the Missouri River flowing through, but the trails in the forest hills remained usable. The floodplain trails were restored over the next few years except for the Walking Club Trail. Several years later, this trail was restored too.

Echoes of Early Footsteps

The whistle of the 1919 interurban, the crackle of film reels—all once-ordinary sounds now resonate as historical markers. Today's walkers tap into those echoes whenever they lace shoes for a Sunday walk and start down familiar paths.

Over the years, the club morphed from a group of post-war adventurers into a close-knit social group. Post-hike meals grew into seasonal festivals combining tennis matches and volleyball with nature walks. Yet these shifts never eclipsed the founding essence: gathering in nature's embrace to learn, to heal, and to celebrate human connection.

A popular World War I-era song captured the spirit of those early years—its lyrics echoing the longing, hope, and companionship that defined the club's beginnings:

There's a long, long trail a-winding
Into the land of my dreams,
Where the nightingales are singing
And a white moon beams:

There's a long, long night of waiting
Until my dreams all come true;

The trail they walked was literal—but also emotional, communal, and enduring. And it still winds forward, carrying their echoes into every new step.

The Unfinished Path

Even as we reflect on the first century, the story is far from complete. The footprints we leave today will guide tomorrow's explorers—whether they hike on a trail, rally for a pickleball volley, or share stories at a winery. The club's unwritten chapters await fresh ink from new voices and new challenges, proving that true legacy is not static but pulses forward with every inspired step.

As the second century has begun, its final invitation is clear: lace your shoes and help write the next verses of this grand odyssey. In doing so, you will join a lineage of walkers and dreamers who have woven their lives into every root and ribbon of trail.

Acknowledgements

This book would not exist in its current form without the generosity and enthusiasm of many people. Thank you to the following individuals and institutions for making it far better than I could have done alone:

Doug Wenger, for contributing a treasure trove of photos, stories, and poems; for reading the draft with a sharp eye; and for restoring some of the photos.

Thomas Rubarth, for unraveling the mysteries of century-old transportation, crafting more readable maps that brought the past to life, suggesting additions to the unadorned back cover of the book, and contributing photos.

Pamela Malley, for hours of idea-bouncing, pointing me toward the right people, and providing historical documents at the very beginning of this journey. Mary Rudy, for beta reading with a fresh perspective and helping me see the book anew.

Catherine Kuper at Fontenelle Forest, for contributing photos and rich information about the forest. Faith and Kori at Sarpy County Museum, for repeatedly hauling out the big totes of Walking Club artifacts—your patience and enthusiasm were invaluable.

Steven and James Morton and Sonja Hauter, for generously sharing family photos. Tom Lazure, for contributing his personal story to the tapestry of club history.

Faith at Washington County Museum, for providing a key photo that helped complete a bio. Michelle at the Omaha World-Herald and Katie at the Durham Museum, for sleuthing through archives to find old photos. Matthew and the front desk team at the Nebraska Historical Society, for locating a personal journal—what a find!

And last, but most important: my husband Jeff, for his unwavering encouragement, for listening to me talk about this book endlessly for three solid months, and for beta reading with love and patience. Your support made all the difference.

Alongside this human chorus of support, I also acknowledge Microsoft Copilot for its limited role in the writing process. The tool offered suggestions for alternative wording and helped smooth paragraph transitions. While Copilot's assistance was meaningful, all research, outlining, substantive content, and creative decisions were entirely my own.

Appendix A –The Walking Club Album

*Shack #1 (ca. 1921) * OWC photo by Ansel Searles*

*"Avenue at Iowa Deaf Institute" 1923 * OWC photo by Rudolph Timmler*

"What's a little barbed wire fence? Nothing say Harriet Mueller and Maude Watson" Omaha Daily Bee, April 17, 1921

*"Scene on E. S. Jewell's Walk" 1924 * OWC photo by R. Timmler*

"C. S. Stebbins & Erval McIlvaine – Our oldest and youngest members"
*1925 * OWC photo by TImmler*

"By the Hollow Tree on the Shack Trail"
*1928 * OWC photo by R. TImmler*

"Hikers at the Forest School"
(ca. 1930) OWC photo

"In the Hills Near Folsom, Iowa"
*1927 * OWC photo by Louise Gwin*

"Walk, Willview to Plattsmouth" April 15,
*1928 * OWC photo by E. S. Jewell*

Walking Club ladies trudging through the snowy forest (ca. 1920)
Photo courtesy of Doug Wenger

"Omaha Walking Club at the Riverside Gun Club Shack on the Platte River" Dec. 16, 1928

*"Around the Campfire" 1926 * OWC photo by Lillie J. Busch*

Hikers in the early years; Edwin Jewell stands on the right side

*"On the Trail Near Honey Creek, Iowa" 1929 * photo by Roy H. Jensen*

King Mountain Hike in 1932

Photos courtesy of Doug Wenger

*Inez (Selander) Coons * photo courtesy of Sonja Hauter*

Hike near the Platte River in January 1933
Photos courtesy of Doug Wenger

Bus Trip to Visit the Hastings Outdoor Club in May 1936
Photos courtesy of Doug Wenger

Cold weather hikes in the early years

Resting during a winter walk
Photos courtesy of Doug Wenger

Cooling off in the 1930's
Photos courtesy of Doug Wenger

Walking Club Tennis Court in 1934

Linoma Beach in 1933

Gypsy Day in 1934

Gypsy Day 1934 was a lively affair, with club members swept into a wild dance. Games followed, led by Nell Baldwin, the gypsy queen. The finale—a Spanish tango performed by Earl Johnson in gaudy feminine attire alongside Ken Wenger—left the crowd roaring with laughter. When the call for "eats" rang out, everyone rushed to line up for gypsy stew, ladled out by Nell and her colorful crew.

Photos courtesy of Doug Wenger

Ralph Andrews (standing), Earl Johnson (on bench), & Ken Wenger (sitting on ground)

Ice Skating on the Missouri River near the Shack

1935 marked the club's first official ice skating winter. Posing in front of newly built wing dams along the Missouri River, members took to the frozen construction zone with enthusiasm—and only a few chilly surprises.

Skaters gather near the Corps of Engineers' wing dams, built to tame the river's flow. Several fell through the ice that season, but with shallow water and quick rescues, the only thing bruised was dignity.

Photos courtesy of Doug Wenger

Walk #654 on March 24, 1935—Honeycreek, Iowa

*Led by Elmer Wenberg, club members hiked the rugged hills from Honeycreek
to Loveland with steady steps and good cheer.*

Photos courtesy of Doug Wenger

Singing round the campfire or the fireplace in the shack (ca. 1934)
Photos courtesy of Doug Wenger

BELOW: Weary hikers pumping water to cool their feet: Mrs. Marchetti, Miss Raph, Rose Poprosky, Adelaine Daley & Mrs. Irma Himebaugh. This pump was the only source of water at the Shack. The water was always cool—even on the hottest days—and had a slight taste of iron in it.

Photos courtesy of Doug Wenger

"Major Bow Wow's Amateur Hour - Station OWC"
Omaha Walking Club's Christmas party at the YWCA building on December 11, 1935
Featuring "The Little Buttercups" (below)
Photos courtesy of Doug Wenger

Appendix B –Fontenelle Forest Map (1944)

*1944 Map of Fontenelle Forest * The Missouri River was channelized in 1938; as a result, the walking club's trail was further away from the river than in the early years. The Boy Scout Camp Gifford was closed and plans were being made for the new Boy Scout Camp on high ground shown near the bottom of the map.*

Appendix C –Streetcar & Interurban Maps

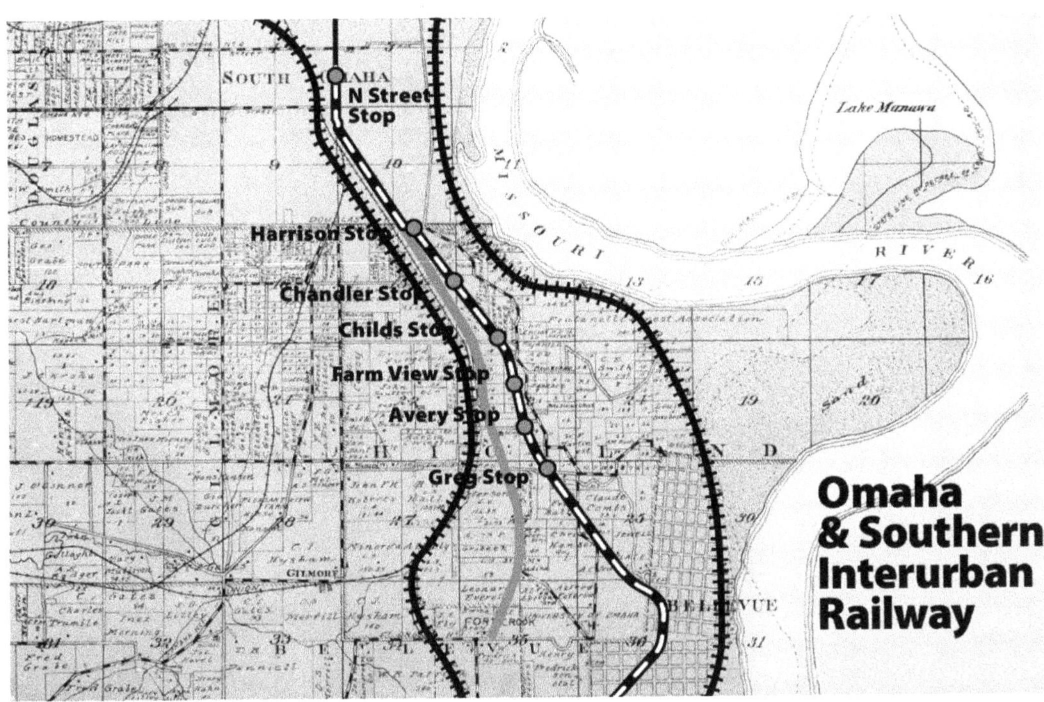

The map on the left shows a section of the metro area in the early years of the Walking Club. Streetcar transportation was widely available at the time. To reach Fontenelle Forest, visitors from Omaha would usually take a streetcar to the southern end of the streetcar route. From there, they would either walk or take the interurban to shorten the walk.

The map on the right shows details of the South Omaha and Bellevue stops.

Maps courtesy of Thomas Rubarth

Appendix D – Members in 1924 (5 years)

Elmo Adams, Margaret Adams, Waldo Adams, L. M. Allen, G. A. Andreen, Hannah M. Andresen, Lillie S. Arlander, Corinne Armstrong,

James Baldwin, Julius F. Baldwin, Nell Baldwin, Bertha M. Barber, John H. Bath, Theodore W. Baumer, Alyce L. Beal, Eva Begley, Mrs. Margaret Benda, S. A. Beranek, Jean Berger, Aloys Berka, Harriet Berry, Mrs. Ida Berry, Louella M. Berry, T. D. Berry, Chelsea M. Besack, Marcus W. Besack, Glenn D. Bevington, Howard H. Biggar, Mrs. Howard Biggar, Mary E. Bird, Margaret Black, May Bothwell, Margaret Boyle, John Oscar Bozell, Leo B. Bozell, Mrs. Leo B. Bozell, Wm. C. Bradford, Margaret Brady, Loretta Brandon, Ida Brigham, J. E. Brill, Mrs. J. E. Brill, David Broadwell, Olga Anne Brodil, Richard Brown, J. T. Buchanan, Mrs. J. T. Buchanan, Frank C. Builta, Ruth Burchert, Roscile Burkhard, Robert E. Burrell, G. A. Burrell, Lillie Jean Busch, Marie Butchi, F. W. Byerly

Nellie L. Christensen, Dr. Wilhelmina Christensen, Gertrude E. Clarke, Ethel E. Cline, Mrs. W. E. Coate, J. H. Coesfeld, Maynard C. Cole, Mrs. Josephine Cook, Wm. Coons, Helen Corr, Judith Corr, Beatrice Cowling, Amy P. Crabbe, Marilla Cudworth,

Ethel Dahlgren, Margaret Davis, Phoebe D. Davis, May Dawson, Fred Deakle, Pauline Devereese, Pearl Dolan, Zaidee Dorsey, Elizabeth Drage, C. F. Drake, Jas. Drummond Jr., Lillian Dubnuff, Nell Duffy, Wm. R. Duffy, Bess I. Dumont, Ann F. Duncan, Mrs. A. K. Egar, Howard Elliott, Mrs. Howard Elliott, Clara Ely, Helen A. Endert, Mabel Engler, Nell Ensor,

Emma Falt, Gaynelle R. Fay, Marguerite Feigel, Joseph P. Ferry, Margaret Flickinger, Chas. E. Foster, Olive Frazer, Vera Freeman, Charles Gadway, Emil Gehrke, Hazel J. Gehrke, Theodore Gehrke, Dr. H. Gifford, Helene B. Gille, Grace Gille, Edward Gisin, Ethel Gordon, Marie Gordon, Mary Louise Guy, Lillian Gwin, Louise M. Gwin,

Harry L. Haberstroh, L. J. Hannan, Eva Harrier, Irene M. Higbee, S. N. Hodes, Mrs. Augusta Hoeg, Edward Homola, Harry P. Hough, Allie H. Houston, Jas. L. Houston, Wm. B. Howard, W. Seavey Hudson, Jennie E. Hultman, P. M. Hummer, Mrs. John H. Hussie, John H. Hussie Jr., Leta Huth,

B. H. Jacobs, Lucile Jalas, Arthur Jeffrey, Clarence E. Jeffrey, Edwin S. Jewell, Ann Johnson, Earl Johnson, Emma Johnson, Howard Johnson, Walter Johnson, Stuart H. Kelly, E. M. Kennedy, Kirby H. Kittoe, Ernest B. Kleburg, L. A. Klein, Emma Kment, Katherine Kocher, Emma Kosumbersky, Chas. Lafferty, Lucille

Larkin, Martin E. Larson, W. B. Larzelere, J. E. Layten, Mrs. J. E. Layten, Mrs. Myron L. Learned, Frank Leslie, Maude Lile, Mrs. Myrtle Lile, Henning J. Lindeman, Lenora Lindsay, Mrs. Audrey Lloyd, Arthur Lyon,

Marie Mackin, Ruth Mackin, Chas. H. Marley, Florence McAllister, Adeline McCulloh, Ina McCurdy, Edward C. McDermott, E. G. McGilton, Erval M. McIlvaine, Mrs. M. F. McIlvaine, Mary B. McIntosh, Loretta McNamara, Maude Miller, Neva Milner, Ernest R. Misner, Dwight Moore, Mrs. Dwight Moore, Eunice Moore, Nell M. Moriarty, Geo. T. Morton, Mrs. Geo. T. Morton, Julia Moylan, Harriet M. Mueller, Ann Theresa Murphy, Thomas B. Murray,

Carl J. Nagy, Mike Nagy, Paul J. Nagy, Bertha Neale, Edith L. Neale, Grace E. Neale, Irene Neligh, Jennie M. Neligh, Mildred D. Neligh, Oscar W. Neligh, Camilla Norris, Elizabeth T. O'Brien, Anna T. Olsson, J. L. Pallat, C. Lois Parkhurst, Elisabeth Parsons, Dr. James M. Patton, Mrs. James M. Patton, Homer F. Pennock, Nancy V. Pennoyer, Cecil Perkins, Lyman O. Perley, Alice L. Peterson, Ethel Pierce, Archie Pjerrou, John C. Pollock, Margaret Power, John R. Proctor,

M. W. Rayley, Julius Reader, N. S. Reeves, Gladys Reeves, Herman G. Reinholz, Mrs. Herman G. Reinholz, Hedvika Reznichek, Polly E. Rhyno, Louise E. Rich, Mabel A. Richardson, John W. Robbins, Mrs. John W. Robbins, Ruth Rockwood, Mrs. Lothar E. Rudolph,

Olga Schermerhorn, M. Ellen Schmidt, Betty Schmitz, Frank Schneider, Joe Schneider, Edward A. Schork, Jennie Sharkey, Rose Shestak, Robert Siegmann, Marjorie Siert, Martin Sitera, June M. Slocum, Rebecca Smith, May Somers, Mabel Spraktes, Edward W. Starr, C. S. Stebbins, Eunice Stebbins, G. P. Stebbins, Irene L. Strong, Pauline Swoboda,

Irene Tauchen, Nadene Thompson, Jack Thomsen, R. Timmler, Edith Tobitt, Mrs. Harriet Tooke, Milin Trentham, Phil M. Trochtenberg, Geo. D. Tunnicliff, Bess C. Turynek, Lydia E. Turynek, Antoinette Uher, E. A. Van Valkenburg, Helen D. Verlantz,

Harry S. Walker, Maude E. Watson, Gus Weist Jr., Joe Weist, Wm. A. Weist, Martha C. Wernimont, Norman J. Weston, Mrs. N. J. Weston, Virginia White, Lewis M. Whitehead, Katherine C. Wilbur, Mrs. John Williams, Leslie F. Williams, Lyman T. Williams, Helen D. Winkelman, R. E. Winkelman, Mrs. R. E. Wilkelman, Alta B. Wolcott, W. I. Wood, Mrs. W. I. Wood, Edith F. Wright, Fred A. Wright, Mrs. Fred Young, Wm. Young, Frances Zadak, Isabel Zigmund, J. J. Zitnik, John Zozaya, Amy Fay Zschau.[1]

Appendix E – Members in 1929 (10 years)

HONORARY MEMBERS:
Dr. Harold Gifford, 3636 Burt St.
Mrs. Sarah Joslyn, 3902 Davenport St.
Roy N. Towl, 506 South 57th St.

Mrs. Lysle Abbott, Elizabeth Adams, Margaret Adams, Mrs. A. Clark Anderson, Grace V. Anderson, Isabel Anderson, Jean Anderson, Hannah M. Andresen, Corinne Armstrong, Stanley M. Atherton,

Nell L. Baldwin, Delsie F. Barker, Norma Barratt, John H. Bath, Mrs. John H. Bath, Leo J. Baum, Alyce L. Beal, Frank H. Becker, Zella C. Beebe, Eva Begley, Vernon C. Bennett, S. A. Beranek, Jean Berger, George J. Berry, Mrs. George J. Berry, A. K. Bettinger, Howard B. Blanchard, Mrs. Howard B. Blanchard, Mrs. Olive C. Booth, Frank Bower, Helen Breiholz, Dorothy Brentlinger, Annie Laurie Brill, David Broadwell, Richard M. Brown, J. T. Buchanan, Mrs. J. T. Buchanan, Frank C. Builta, Mrs. Frank C. Builta, Raymond J. Burke, Mary Burns, G. A. Burrell, Mrs. G. A. Burrell, Lillie Jean Busch, Charlotte Buttler,

Mildred L. Califf, Richard C. Claybaugh, Albert L. Cockle, J. H. Coesfeld, Winnie Coffey, William A. Coons, Mrs. William A. Coons, Amy P. Crabbe, M. Hazel Crandall, Viva Anne Craven, Warren Creel, A. I. Creigh, Mrs. A. I Creigh, Lucile Cromwall, Faye Curtis, Frances Curtis, G. Urban Curtis,

Ethel Dahlgren, Fred A. Deakle, Mrs. Fred A. Deakle, Pauline Devereese, Ruth Downs, C. F. Drake, Minniejane Drey, Bess I. Dumont, Ann F. Duncan, Dr. A. A. Edginton, Beth Ellington, Ethel G. Eldridge, Helen A. Endert, Gaynelle R. Fay, E. A. Fitzpatrick, A. N. Fogelstrom, Mrs. Albert Foll, Chas. E. Foster, E. B. Fowler, Vera A. Fuller,

Charles Gadway, Mrs. Charles Gadway, Frank H. Garvin, Grace Gille, Helene Gille, Edward Gisin, Mary Gleason, Clara Glock, Della Lee Gowen, R. B. Gray, Mrs. R. B. Gray, Lillian Gwin, Louise M. Gwin,

Harry Haberstroh, Ora R. Hamilson, Clarence Hansen, Gilbert C. Harry, Mrs. Gilbert C. Harry, Mary Hart, Anne M. Haskin, Hough Haskins, Florence Hawley, Mrs. C. M. Hensky, Marvelle Hensky, R. W. Herrmann, Irene M. Higbee, Howard L. Hite, Jean T. Hobart, S. N. Hodes, Harry P. Hough, Mrs. Harry P. Hough, Allie H. Houston, August Huenecke, Lincoln V. Hughes, Ollie Hughes, Paul M. Hummer, Mrs. Paul M. Hummer, Vincent H. Hunter, Mrs. Vincent H. Hunter,

Mary Catherine Jack, Helene Janicek, Annetta Jensen, Celia Jensen, Roy H. Hensen, Edwin S. Jewell, Earl R. Johnson, Mrs. Earl R. Johnson, Howard Johnson, Dorothy Johnston, William Jones, Edward Kahn, Elizabeth Kaufman, E. M. Kennedy, Ethel Ketcham, Mrs. Ernest Kleburg, Charles J. Klina, Emma Kosumbersky,

Junior Landworth, J. F. Lawless, James E. Layten, Eleanor Jane Lear, Wm. Ledoux, Frank Leslie, Mrs. Frank Leslie, Gladys Lindberg, Waldo H. Longnecker, Margaret Lucid, Flossie Lyons, Verda Lytton, Phyllis McCarron, Theresa McGee, E. G. McGilton, Helen L. Mackin, Geo. A. Marsh, Mrs. Geo. A. Marsh, Alice Marhall, Minnie May, Harold L. Meier, Henry G. Meyer, Dorothy Meyers, Grace A. Mickel, James Moran, Mrs. C. J. Morton, Geo. T. Morton, Mrs. Geo. T. Morton, Harriet M. Mueller, Helen Muenchrath, Lily B. Munro, Thos. B. Murray, Ann Myers,

Carl J. Nagy, Jennie M. Neligh, Thea Estelle Nelson, Mrs. Merle New, Grace Nickell, Eva M. Nielsen, John J. H. Oehlrich, Gabriel Olech, Anna T. Olsson, Leah H. Osborn, Homer F. Pennock, Archie Pjerrou, John R. Proctor, Mrs. John R. Proctor, Mary Prokop, Mary C. Quinby, Polly E. Ryhno, Anna M. Robertson, Mrs. John W. Robbins, Gladys Rye, Irene Rubin,

Eva Sanders, Robert Sandes, Vernon Sandes, M. Ellen Schmidt, Walter Schopp, Minta Schurr, Gladys J. Shamp, Gertrude Shanahan, Jennie Sharkey, Mabel Shatwell, Lili Reed Showalter, Ada Elizabeth Smith, Bertha A. Smith, Mrs. Ruth Smith, Suzanne Smith, W. T. Smith, Mrs. W. T. Smith, Mrs. Max Sommer, Mrs. L. Evelyn Sorensen, Lillian Sorensen, Tom M. Staley, Louise Stegner, Elfie L. Swanson,

Irene B. Tauchen, Mrs. Opal Thurber Jr., Rudolph Timmler, Geo. D. Tunnicliff, Mrs. Geo. D. Tunnicliff, A. F. Turynek, Bess C. Turynek, Douglas Van Valkenburgh, E. A. Van Valkenburgh, Mrs. Maud Lile Walker, Jessie B. Watson, Earl R. Wedberg, Herman Weist, Joe Weist, E. A. Wenberg, R. H. Wensberg, Mrs. R. H. Wensberg, Leslie F. Williams, Mrs. Leslie F. Williams, Lyman T. Williams, R. E. Winkelman, Mrs. R. E. Winkelman, Richard A. Winn, Amy Woodruff, Isabel Zigmund.[1]

Appendix F – Members in 1944 (25 years)

Sigrid Anderson '43, Hannah Andresen '29, Frances Axtell '30, Nell Baldwin '21, Della Bowers '44, Edna Braun '38, Al Brielmaier '43, Pvt. Robert D. Bruce '42, Alice A. Burke '36, Joseph J. Burke '34, Mildred Burke '30, Raymond Burke '28, G. A. Burrell '22, Lillie Jean Busch '20, Dorothy Butterworth '33,

T/3 Roy Carlson '41, S/Sgt. Lloyd Clayton '38, J. J. Collins '43, Pfc. George Cousens '30, Ruth Dahl '41, Bess Dumont '19, Chauncey Evans '30, Harry C. Finney '41, A. N. Fogelstrom '29, Ruth Frohardt '44, Mrs. Charles Gadway '29, Charles Gadway '21, Maurine Gamble '44, Edward Gisin '21, Helen Graham '41, Stanley W. Guzal '42,

Maxine Hammack '41, Jean Harper '42, Gilbert C. Harry '25, Harold H. Hatch '35, R. W. Herrmann '30, Irene Higbee '19, Bernice Hofmann '30, Edith Holdorf '43, Cpl. Ella Hornig '36, Clifford F. Hultgren '37, Dorothy Jetter '40, Ellouise Jetter '40, Mary Lou Johnson '26, Earl R. Johnson '21,

Pvt. Edward J. Karlik '42, Marjorie King '42, Ensign Clifford C. King '41, Isabel Kusleka '21, William HA 2/c Little '43, Patrick HA 2/c Maas '42, Marjorie Marchetti '39, Lt. P. E. Marchetti '39, Lt. Carl Markkanen '40, Betty McCracken '44, Celeste McCurdy '31, Sgt. Donald W. Metcalfe '41, Adeline Mix '44, Dorothy Mortensen '43,

Dr. O. W. Neligh '22, Harry R. Nelson '36, Vincent E. Nelson '43, Helen Nestle '41, Stanley A. Nestle '41, Leah H. Osborn '25, Vera Olson '36, Lillian Pavlik '40, Mildred Pavlik '40, Elizabeth Pinkerton '43,

Raymond A. Ramey '29, Vera F. Ramey '28, F. W. Retz C. M. M. '43, Mrs. F. W. Retz '43, Dorothy Rice '33, Ruth Richling '40, Lt. Theodore L. Richling '40, Hugh C. Robertson '44, Louella Roberts '41, 1st Sgt. Stephen H. Roberts '38, George C. Rothery '35, Herman G. Rusch '40,

Henrietta Schoon '41, Blanche Schroeder '30, Minta Schurr '31, Jennie Sharkey '21, George L. S 2/c Skrivanek '42, S/Sgt. Orville W. Smith '40, Grace Smith

'40, Roger C. Spiegel '42, Florence Taylor '32, Ruth Thomas '39, A/C Allan H. Trant '44, Mary Lou Trant '43, Iva Trant '43, S. R. Trans '43, Bess Turynek '21,

J. O. Vanek '30, Robert E. Vokolek '32, Frances Ward '33, Ruth Weddle '40, Doris Wenger '36, Lt. K. C. Wenger '31, Grace Wenberg '22, Elmer A. Wenberg '28, Mildred Williams '24, Lyman T. Williams '20, R. E. Winkelman '19, Julius J. Zitnik '21.[1]

Appendix G – Members in 1969 (50 years)

The year the member joined follows each name.
Marilynn Andersen '48, Hannah M. Andreson '29, Mrs. Augusta Aulabaugh '67, Robert D. Barton '51, Ruth M. Beckman '39, Lillian M. Benak '44, Emil C. Bolton '61, Mrs. Emily Bolton '61, Rudy Brazda '65, Mrs. Marie Brazda '65, Mrs. Jeanne Brown '69, Mrs. N. Fern Buis '67, Joseph Burke '34, Mrs. Alice Burke '36, Lloyd Clayton '38, Mrs. Gloria Clayton '46, Edward Collins '58, William Coons '21, Mrs. Inez Coons '24, Elizabeth A. Costello '55, Harold Courtier '55, Mrs. Louise Cunningham '66, Mrs. Elaine Davey '69, C. C. Day '46, Mrs. Dorothy Day '33, Henrietta DeBoer '65, James DeVaney '59, Mrs. Mary DeVaney '48, John Deveroux '31, Mrs. Clover Deveroux '31, Mrs. Sheila Dinsmore '62, Ethel Doerr '67, Margaret Dorsey '48, Willis B. Duffy '46, Mrs. Julia Duffy '52,

Velma Ellithorpe '68, Ellen Epperson '68, Mrs. Helen Ericksen '51, Mrs. Betty Eskesen '67, Mrs. Frances Evans '30, Robert C. Felker '67, Frank Fenger '68, Mrs. Elizabeth Fonger '66, Dr. Donald Max Fitch '46, Mrs. Helen Fogelstrom '48, Charley Gadway '21, Mrs. Harriet Gadway '22, George Gengler '68, Mrs. Lois Gibson '57, Barbara M. Gilbert '68, Fred Gilbert '63, Mrs. Warda Gilbert '63, Karl Glanzel '63, Mrs. Hilda Glanzel '63, Dorothy A. Gliva '68, Mary Goeser '67, Mary Hackman '63, Alice Hagg '53, Lorene M. Hanna '63, Hugh Harp '68, Mrs. Rita Harp '68, Gilbert C. Harry '25, Mary Hart '50, Harold H. Hatch '35, Mrs. Ramona Hayes '46, Leone Hegge '51, Leland Henningsen '57, Mrs. Mary Heyer '62, Mrs. Johanna Hoff '63, Louise Hoffman '68, Mrs. Ruth Horacek '68, Stephen Horn '58, Mrs. Janie Horn '65, Allie H. Houston '19, Mabel Hrabik '45, Mrs. Mabel Huff '69, Lincoln V. Hughes '27,

H. A. Jacobberger II '67, Frances Jasa '69, Don Jefferson '60, Mrs. Rose Jefferson '60, Donald Jefferson '65, Howard J. Jensen '53, Edward C. Johnson '68, Mrs. Eloyse Johnson '68, Willard Johnson '68, Albert Joseph '53, Mrs. Ella Hornig Joseph '36, Dr. Gustav Kaldegg '63, Mrs. Erna Kaldegg 64, Mrs. Carolyn Kilburn '61, Al Koch '37, Mrs. Vera Olson Koch '36, Simon Koenig '58, Mrs. Anne Koenig '58, John J. Kovarik '61, John F. Kovarik Sr. '66, Tom Kovarik '67, Margaret Krause '61, Joseph Kriz '67, Mrs. Margaret Kriz '67, Martha Kundy '53, Frank LaFerla '67, Mrs. Bernadette LaFerla '67, Charles L. Lamson Jr. '61, Lyle Lander '48, Mrs. Lela Lander '53, Charles E. Lazure '47, Charles B. Lazure '68, John P. Lazure '45, Philip A. Lazure '47, Mrs. Olive M. Lewis '55,

Walter E. McEveny '58, Charles Mach '49, Mrs. Marian Mach '52, Denton P. Maggard '65, Peter E. Marchetti '39, Mrs. Marjorie Marchetti '39, Mrs. Ludmila Matys '66, Stanley Micek '55, Mrs. Doris Micek '55, Mrs. Gertrude Micek '67, Michael Micek '64, Mrs. Sandra Micek '67, Ruth Millard '62, Warren Gene Miner '49, Tom P. Moore '59, Mrs. Mary Morinelli '62, Mary Ann Muenchrath 68,

Dr. Allen Nachman '64, Thor L. Nelson '38, Mrs. Lillian. Nelson, Mrs. Ada Nielsen '46, Mrs. Martha O'Malley '63, Mrs. Ruth Orwick '67, Joe Pavlik '61, Mrs. Frances Pavlik '61, Mrs. Marion Peterson '68, Carmen Polan '66, Mrs. Marie Praetorius '45, Frank J. Pros '68, Mrs. Aurelia Pros '68,

Leni Rauschenberg '48, Ted Richling '40, Mrs. Harriet Riek '67, Mrs. Rose Rizzuto '61, Mrs. Mildred Root '52, Kenneth Schmidt '67, Mrs. Shirley Schmidt '67, Mrs. Bernice Schutz '48, Mrs. Ruth Senter '60, Al K. Sherbondy '58, Mrs. Clara Sherbondy '58, Joseph Shimek '58, Mrs. Nell Shimek '58, Mrs. Corinne Smith '65, Catherine Spenner '64, James Spicka '65, Ray Spicka '64, Mrs. Marjorie Spicka '64, John Squiers '67, Mrs. Nancy Squiers '67, Mrs. Rachel H. Stanford '66, Mrs. Margarette Starkey '69, Carl H. Steinhaus '55, Mrs. Ann Steinhaus '33, John Straka 64, Mrs. Wilhelmina Straka '58, Nancy Straub '69, Hyacinth Suing '61, Susanne Surber '66, Warren Swigart '66, Mrs. Rita Swigart '68, Josephine Switzer '58,

Florence Taylor '32, Mrs. Monica Taylor '64, Leslie Thiessen '68, Mrs. Ingeborg Thiessen '68, Mrs. Henrietta Thomas '61, Jacob Trautrimas '56, Mrs. Rita D. Traynor '68, Mrs. Helen M. Turner '54, Helen Tvrdy '46,

Mrs. Bessie J. Van Deusen '67, Charles Vaugier '62, Mrs. Lillian Vesiak '40, Robert Vokolek '32, Carl Wallin '49, Ruth M. Weddle '40, Ethel Weir '56, Jane C. Weiss '63, Kenneth C. Wenger '31, Mrs. Doris Wenger '36, Barbara Wenger '66, Judy Wenger '66, Mrs. Isabelle Wenzl '61, Everett Wilber '62, Mrs. Kathleen Wilber '62, Lyman T. Williams '20, Mrs. Mildred Williams '24, Mrs. Saundra Wilson '66, Mrs. Mildred Womack '40, Doris Wotherspoon '55, William G. Ziegler '51, Mrs. Elloise Ziegler '40.[1]

Appendix H – List of Club Presidents

1919 Edith Tobitt
1920 Edwin S. Jewell
1921 Allie Houston
1922 Harriet Mueller
1923 Leslie Williams
1924 Norman Weston
    Irene Higbee
1925 Corrinne Armstrong
1926 Earl R. Johnson
1927 Roy B. Gray
1928 R. E. Winkelman
1929 Lyman T. Williams
1930 Gus A. Burrell
1931 Fred A. Deakle
1932 Earl R. Johnson
1933 Raymond A. Ramey
1934 Edwin S. Jewell
1935 R. L. Nesbit
1936 Kenneth C. Wenger
1937 Joseph J. Burke
1938 D. C. Olmstead
1939 Joseph J. Burke
1940 J. R. Bethune
1941 George Cousens
1942 Peter E. Marchetti
1943 Harry C. Finney
1944 Earl R. Johnson
1945 Joseph J. Burke
1946 Ruth M. Weddle
1947 Lloyd Clayton
1948 Charley E. Gadway
1949 John Devereux
1950 C. C. Day
1951 Dorothy Day
1952 Charley E. Gadway
1953 Carl I. Wallin
1954 Lyle C. Lander
1955 John P. Lazure
1956 Ruth M. Beckman

1957 Kenneth C. Wenger
1958 Herman Huser
1959 Margaret Dorcey
1960 Harry R. Nelson
1961 Dr. Donald M. Fitch
1962 Stanley F. Micek
1963 Don Jefferson
1964 Albert E. Joseph
1965 John K. Jovardy
1966 Al K. Sherbondy
1967 Hyacinth Suing
1968 Elizabeth Costello
1969 Kenneth C. Wenger
1970 Don Jefferson
1971 Warren G. Miner
1972 Robert E. Felker
1973 John I. Straka
1974 Kenneth A. Schmidt
1975 Ted Nickerson
1976 Charles E. Lazure
1977 A. Burd Argabright
1978 Margaret Dorcey
1979 Joseph J. Burke
1980 Alice Hagg
1981 Nell Simpkins
1982 Dr. Donald M. Fitch
    Elizabeth Costello
1983 Elizabeth Costello
1984 Monroe G. Evans
1985 A. Burd Arganbright
1986 John P. Lazure
1987 Hyacinth Suing
1988 Rita Eldrige
1989 Dave Garrison
1990 Alice Hagg
1991 Eloise Evans
1992 John P. Lazure
1993 Elizabeth Costello
1994 A. Burd Arganbright

1995 A. Burd Arganbright
1996 Muriel Munchrath
1997 Murial Munchrath
1998 Bill Anderson
1999 Bill Anderson
2000 Gary Bonner
2001 Wayne Lainof
2002 Wayne Lainof
2003 Mark Thomas
2004 Dave Garrison
2005 Chuck Lazure
2006 Glenn Beedon
2007 Glenn Beedon
2008 (position open)
2009 Dave Garrison
2010 Thomas Schulte
2011 Thomas Schulte
2012 Thomas Schulte
2013 Judy Alderman
2014 Judy Alderman
2015 Judy Alderman
2016 Dave Garrison
2017 Judy Alderman
2018 Pamela Malley
2019 Pamela Malley
2020 Cathy Pakiz
2021 Cathy Pakiz
2022 William Moninger
2023 William Moninger
2024 William Moninger
2025 Clare Gertsch &
    Susan Matzen

References

[1] Omaha Walking Club Collection at Sarpy County Museum

[2] "The Omaha Walking Club Handbook" Collection

[3] "Omaha Walking Club Yearbook" Collection

[4] "Beauties About Omaha Develop a New Local Institution—The Walking Club," *Omaha World-Herald*, May 25, 1919, p 54

[5] "Omaha Walking Club Resumes Hikes in Month," *Sunday World-Herald*, August 24, 1919, p 7

[6] *The Omaha Daily News*, December 7, 1919, p 8

[7] "Walking Club Elects," *Evening World-Herald*, January 15, 1920, p 12

[8] "Just a Mean Old Knicker-Snicker," *Evening World-Herald*, August 13, 1938, p 2

[9] "Omaha Walking Club Elects New Officers," *Omaha Daily News*, January 12, 1921, p 8

[10] "Weekend Parties are Very Popular," *Omaha World-Herald*, August 20, 1922, p 34

[11] "Progress of Walking Club Noted at the Tenth Annual Celebration," *Omaha World-Herald*, March 29, 1929, p 22

[12] "Club House Redecorated," *Omaha World-Herald*, June 25, 1934, p 13

[13] Doug Wenger and the collection of Ken & Doris Wenger

[14] "25th Year Marked by Walking Club," *Evening World-Herald*, December 8, 1944, p 11

[15] "Omaha Walking Club Still Walks," *Omaha World-Herald*, June 9, 1946, p 56

[16] "Club to Retrace Original Steps 50 Years Later," *Omaha World-Herald*, March 16, 1969, p 81

[17] "Walking Club Visits Ranch," *The Grand Island Independent*, September 8, 1971, p 17

[18] "49 Get Awards of Walking Club," *Omaha World-Herald*, May 18, 1979, p 38

[19] Fontenelle Forest

[20] Wikipedia

[21] "Focus on Fontenelle Forest," *Omaha World-Herald*, January 23, 1975, p 17

[22] Gary Garabrandt, "The Story of Fontenelle Forest," a chapter in Jerold L. Simmons, Ph.D., La Belle Vue: Studies in the History of Bellevue, Nebraska, 1976

[23] "Another Big Stride," *Omaha World-Herald*, July 12, 1919, p 14

[24] "New Boy Scouts Camp is Ready," *Evening World-Herald*, June 5, 1947, p 25

[25] Nebraska Department of Natural Resources

[26] "Hikers Must Look After 'Chores'," *Evening World-Herald*, February 22, 1921, p 8

[27] "Walking Club Hut in Woods Burns Down," *Evening World-Herald*, May 27, 1921, p 8

[28] "All the World Loves a Fireplace," *Omaha Daily Bee*, September 11, 1921, p 9

[29] "Walking Club has 150 on Sunday Hike," *Evening World-Herald*, October 17, 1921, p 4

[30] "Walking Club Delays Homecoming Event," *Evening World-Herald*, April 10, 1943, p 8

[31] Club member Dave Garrison

[32] Educational Service Unit #3

[33] "Walking Club Can't Keep Buildings on Forest's Edge," *Omaha World-Herald*, July 26, 1992, p 33

[34] Douglas County Historical Society

[35] Nebraskaland Magazine, December 26, 2022

[36] U.S. Federal Census

[37] Omaha Public Library

[38] "Edith Tobitt is Dead at 71," *Omaha World-Herald*, July 6, 1939, p 6

[39] "Morton-Hendrie Wedding," *Omaha Evening Bee*, June 19, 1916, p 13

[40] "Mrs. George T. Morton Dead," *Omaha World-Herald*, February 23, 1910, p 5

[41] Nebraska U.S. Birth Ledgers

[42] "Omaha Walking Club Party to Leave Saturday for Outing," *Omaha Daily News*, July 16, 1926, p 8

[43] James Morton

[44] "Fontenelle Forest Men are Enthusiastic," *Evening World-Herald*, January 15, 1919, p 8

[45] "Outdoors from Week to Week," *Omaha World-Herald*, September 11, 1921, p 32

[46] "Hikers Return from Estes Park," *Omaha Daily News*, August 1, 1921, p 3

[47] "Omaha Woman's Club," *Omaha Daily Bee*, February 9, 1919, p 25

[48] "E. S. Jewell Dies at Desk," *Evening World-Herald*, December 4, 1941, p 28

[49] "Forestry Foundation Approved by Group," *Evening World-Herald*, April 9, 1941, p 4

[50] Erin Torell, "UNMC history: The dynamic and generous Dr. Gifford", *University of Nebraska Medical Center*, 2024

[51] Find A Grave

[52] "Canoe Hikers Dock at K.C.," *Omaha Morning Bee News*, April 19, 1930, p 9

[53] "Leo Bozell Ad Man Dies," *Evening World-Herald*, March 25, 1946, p 16

[54] "Lois Robbins Bride of Leo Bozell Today," *Omaha Daily News*, August 20, 1921, p 7

[55] "Love for Pioneers Directed Her Life," *Omaha World-Herald*, March 2, 1975, p 65

[56] "Walking Club Plans Two Hikes," *Evening World-Herald*, July 3, 1923, p 4

[57] "Hike at Ft. Calhoun," *Omaha World-Herald*, March 25, 1934, p 26

[58] *Omaha World-Herald*, November 9, 1935, p 10

[59] "Benefactor Miss Neale to have Tuesday Rite," *Omaha World-Herald*, May 23, 1980, p 38

[60] "Omaha Walking Club Bulletin" Collection

[61] "Hikers Stroll Through Child's Point District," *Evening World-Herald*, April 21, 1919, p 5

[62] *Evening World-Herald*, April 28, 1919, p 2

[63] Hack, Wolf, Gunderson. "Robert Fletcher Gilder: Archeologist for the Museum." Digital Commons@University of Nebraska-Lincoln.

[64] Ben Justman, "Images of America: Bellevue," 2011

[65] "One Hike Only During July," *Omaha World-Herald*, July 1, 1923, p 37

[66] "Omaha Walking Club," *Omaha Daily News*, November 16, 1919, p 28

[67] "Clubs," *Omaha Daily News*, November 7, 1920, p 17

[68] "Omaha Walking Club Has Varied Program Planned," *Omaha World-Herald*, January 1, 1922, p 18

[69] "Three Women Take Part in Endurance Walk of Twenty-five Miles," *Evening World-Herald*, January 17, 1922, p 8

[70] "85-Year-Old Sets Hike Pace," *Omaha World-Herald*, November 23, 1969, p 32

[71] "Veteran Hikers Find Sport Gaining Fans," *Omaha World-Herald*, November 29, 1974, p 1

[72] "Woman Walks from Omaha to Nemaha via Auburn," *Nemaha County Herald*, April 2, 1926, p 6

[73] Newspaper archives

[74] "Eight Members of Omaha Walking Club Here Sunday," *Nebraska Daily News Press*, May 23, 1922, p 2

[75] *The Gretna Breeze*, October 27, 1922, p 4

[76] "Omaha Lovers of the Out-of-Doors Plan Early Morning Breakfast Hikes," *Omaha Daily News*, April 9, 1921, p 5

[77] "Midnight-to-Sunrise Hike is Scheduled," *Omaha World-Herald*, November 16, 1934, p 20

[78] "Above River, they Run, Walk and Rock," *Omaha World-Herald*, September 29, 2008, p 1-2

[79] "A Child Shall Lead Them," *Omaha Evening Bee*, March 25, 1921, p 13

[80] "On 90th Birthday, Pops Takes a Long Walk—to a Party," *Omaha World-Herald*, February 18, 1974, p 1

[81] "Police Judge Quits Bench and Becomes Official Steak Roaster for Tramp Band," *Omaha Evening Bee*, April 11, 1921, p 2

[82] "Walking Club to have Picnic," *Omaha World-Herald*, October 10, 1926, p 42

[83] "Omaha Walking Club Has Outing, Breakfast Sunday," *Evening World-Herald*, March 14, 1938, p 13

[84] "Omaha Walking Club to Entertain Saturday," *Evening World-Herald*, October 28, 1926, p 14

85 "Omaha Walking Club of School Teachers to take Long Hikes," *Omaha Daily Bee*, November 27, 1919, p 4

86 "Bring 'Useless' Gift Says Notice," *Omaha World-Herald*, December 17, 1922, p 17

87 "Walking Club will Negotiate 'Mountains' of Council Bluffs," *Omaha World-Herald*, December 28, 1919, p 32

88 "Walking Club Entertains," *Omaha World-Herald*, December 31, 1922, p 19

89 *Omaha World-Herald*, January 1, 1924, p 14

90 *Omaha World-Herald*, May 13, 1919, p 2

91 "Breakfast for those who go to Mountains," *Omaha World-Herald*, June 28, 1925, p 34

92 "Walking Club Events," *Omaha World-Herald*, July 3, 1927, p 27

93 "Walking Club will Dance—Not Walk," *Omaha World-Herald*, February 4, 1923, p 59

94 "The Omaha Walking Club," *Omaha Evening Bee*, February 3, 1922, p 5

95 "Hike will end in May-Pole Dance," *Evening World-Herald*, May 25, 1923, p 20

96 "Walking Club to Picnic at Krug Park," *Omaha Daily Bee*, June 24, 1923, p 27

97 "Walking Club Skating Party," *Evening World-Herald*, January 25, 1940, p 8

98 "Hikers Hold Dance," *Omaha World-Herald*, October 26, 1935, p 12

99 "Square Dance Slated," *Evening World-Herald*, June 1, 1956, p 25

100 "Hikers Planning Saturday Outing," *Evening World-Herald*, October 29, 1957, p 10

101 "Ever Hear of a Pictorialist?" *Omaha World-Herald*, March 16, 1930, p 57

102 "Mt. Whitney, Death Valley Day's Work for Bill Coons," *South Omaha Sun*, August 12, 1954, p 18

103 "W. A. Coons Dead at 71; Funeral will be Friday," *Omaha World-Herald*, April 8, 1976, p 50

104 "Society," *Omaha Evening Bee*, August 4, 1921, p 9

105 "Treacherous Bog Crossed by Two of Walking Club," *Omaha Evening Bee*, August 28, 1922, p 1

106 "Walking Club have Gala Time on Black Hills Trip," *Evening World-Herald*, July 23, 1923, p 6

107 "St. Paul Hikers Greet Members of Local Club," *Evening World-Herald*, August 23, 1923, p 11

108 "Take 205-Mile Jaunt in Glacier Park," *Omaha Daily News*, August 8, 1923, p 8

109 "Lake Jewell Named in Honor of Walking Club Organizer," *Omaha Daily News*, August 9, 1924, p 1

110 "Omaha Walking Club Mountain Outing," *Omaha Evening Bee*, May 30, 1924, p 5

111 "The Walking Club Gypsies," *Evening World-Herald*, August 20, 1924, p 8

112 "Walking Club Members Return," *Omaha World-Herald*, July 28, 1925, p 5

113 "Omaha Walking Club Will Climb Cloud's Peak in Big Horn Mountains," *Stockman's Journal*, July 17, 1926, p 2

114 "Into the Big Horn Mountains on Foot," *Omaha Daily Bee*, September 5, 1926, p 41

115 "Walking Club Plans Outing Lake Iwaqua," *Omaha World-Herald*, May 17, 1925, p 17

116 "Club Rides, Rides, Rides to Walk, Walk, Walk," *Evening World-Herald*, September 2, 1950, p 8

117 "Hiking Club Visits Ranch," *Telegraph*, September 9, 1971, p 3

118 "Four Teams Win Into Spiker Playoffs at Y," *Omaha World-Herald*, April 13, 1935, p 14

119 "Woodbine Wins 'Y' Volley Title," *Omaha Sunday Bee News*, April 14, 1935, p 11

120 "Benson Captures Volleyball Title," *Omaha Evening Bee News*, April 17, 1936, p 24

121 "Locals Lick Omaha Volleyball Girls," *Daily Nonpareil*, January 19, 1938, p 11

122 "Benson Gal Spikers Cop," *Omaha World-Herald*, February 2, 1938, p 13

123 "Recreation Team Wins," *Evening World-Herald*, October 19, 1939, p 18

124 "O. A. C. Men Take Hot Volleyball Battle," *Omaha World-Herald*, November 15, 1939, p15

125 "Volleyball Matches to 'Y,' Benson Teams, *Evening World-Herald*, December 7, 1939, p 27

126 "J. C. C. Spikers Win," *Evening World-Herald*, December 8, 1939, p 33

127 "Breakfast at Shack," *Omaha World-Herald*, April 19, 1937, p 4

[128] "Walkers Will Use Canoes," *Omaha World-Herald*, October 1, 1922, p 17

[129] "Will Take an Endurance Walk," *Omaha World-Herald*, October 28, 1923, p 35

[130] "Omaha Couples Emulate Gertrude Edrerle; Swim 20 Miles in Missouri," *Omaha Daily News*, August 25, 1925, p 11

[131] "Eager to Swim but the Missouri Ice was too Thick," *Omaha World-Herald*, March 3, 1930, p 7

[132] "'Skippers' Ply Missouri on Rafts," *Omaha Daily Bee*, September 9, 1923, p 12

[133] "Walkers Paddle 40 Miles on River," *Omaha Evening Bee*, September 16, 1925, p 1

[134] "Voyageurs on River," *Omaha World-Herald*, September 25, 1926, p 28

[135] "Travel Shaveless and Shoeless," *Omaha Morning Bee*, July 4, 1927, p 1

[136] "Omahans in Long Voyage," *Omaha World-Herald*, August 8, 1930, p 17

[137] "Canoeists End 6-Week Trip to Omaha from Headwaters of Missouri River," *Omaha World-Herald*, September 8, 1930, p 2

[138] "Bird Societies will have Joint Meeting," *Evening World-Herald*, May 3, 1921, p 2

[139] "Dr. Gifford Relates Some of His Experiences on Visit to Tropics," *Omaha World-Herald*, May 14, 1921, p 2

[140] "Walking Club Sponsors Recital," *Omaha World-Herald*, February 26, 1922, p 35

[141] *Our Sunday Visitor*, March 10, 1922, p 8

[142] "Calendar of Week," *Omaha Sunday Bee-News*, October 18, 1931, p 23

[143] "Omaha Walking Club to Hike North of Florence," *The Weekly Gateway*, October 3, 1922, p 1

[144] "Eureka Club to Have Hike," *South Omaha Sun*, April 11, 1928, p 1

[145] "Outdoor Club has 27 Omaha Guests," *Hastings Daily Tribune*, May 27, 1933, p 2

[146] "Sioux City Hikers Guests of Omaha Walking Club," *Omaha Evening Bee News*, November 1, 1934, p 12

[147] "Walking Club Luncheon Honors Miss Grace Ficken," *Omaha Evening Bee News*, June 14, 1935, p 12

[148] "Byxbe to Tell Club About Drypoint Work," *Omaha Sunday Bee-News*, October 11, 1931, p 23

[149] "Week's Activities of the Business and Professional Women's Clubs of State," *Lincoln Journal Star*, May 30, 1926, p 30

[150] "Two Clubs Meet at Arbor Lodge," *Nebraska City News Press*, September 8, 1926, p 3

[151] *Evening World-Herald*, November 4, 1926, p 14

[152] "K. of C. Club to Hike," *Omaha Morning Bee News*, October 25, 1934, p 19

[153] "Party, Hike Planned for Omaha U. Women," *Omaha World-Herald*, October 25, 1933, p 18

[154] "J. C. C. Women Hike," *Omaha World-Herald*, April 17, 1932, p 21

[155] "League of Youth on Fontenelle Hike Tonight," *Omaha Evening Bee News*, September 1, 1933, p 10

[156] "Girls Hike Sunday," *South Omaha Sun*, April 10, 1934, p 2

[157] "Omahans Guests," *Lincoln Journal Star*, June 6, 1938, p 9

[158] "Wonder of Peace Impressed on Fontenelle Forest Hikers," *Omaha World-Herald*, May 26, 1940, p 10

[159] "Omaha Hiking Club to Entertain for Touring Minneapolis Group," *Omaha World-Herald*, July 13, 1941, p 45

[160] "Club to Study Flowers in Fontenelle Forest," *Omaha World-Herald*, April 27, 1947, p 57

[161] "Dubuque Group Visits Omaha Walking Club," *Omaha World-Herald*, March 27, 1949, p 1

[162] "Walking Club Host to Forest Trusstees," *Omaha World-Herald*, May 8, 1949, p 12

[163] "Club Took Many Trips," *Omaha World-Herald*, March 5, 1950, p 77

[164] "Sunday Hike Planned by Lutheran Couples," *Omaha World-Herald*, May 22, 1970, p 20

[165] "6-Inch Snow Helps Grain; Plane Down," *Omaha Evening Bee News*, February 25, 1929, p 1

[166] "Plane Forced Down," *Omaha World-Herald*, February 25, 1929, p 1

[167] "Volunteers Spend Sunday Working at Child's Point," *Omaha World-Herald*, August 21, 1922, p 2

[168] *Omaha Evening Bee News*, August 16, 1932, p 16

[169] *Star-Herald (Scottsbluff)*, April 21, 1949, p 13

[170] "Fontenelle Forest Fire Breaks Out Frequently," *Papillion Times*, November 12, 1953, p 1

[171] "Blaze Blackens More Than 300 Acres Near Bellevue," *Evening World-Herald*, April 11, 1956, p 22

[172] "Chain-Call Alarm System Averts Disaster at Forest," *Evening World-Herald*, May 5, 1966, p 3

[173] Gary Garabrandt's notes from an interview with John Baldwin on May 22, 1979

[174] "Hermit Likes Kids, Hates Increased Taxes," *Omaha World-Herald*, August 1, 1954, p 18

[175] "Old Jim May Be a Hermit, but He's Not Anti-Social," *Bellevue Press*, July 24, 1959, p 10

[176] "Who Was Jim Baldwin?" *Omaha World-Herald*, June 24, 1972, p 4

[177] "Ft. Crook Students Bring Day of Thanks Closer for Many Needy Individuals," *Sarpy County Gazette*, November 29, 1960, p 6

[178] "Legion Auxiliary," *Bellevue Press*, December 30, 1960, p 8

[179] *Bellevue Press*, June 3, 1960, p 3

[180] "What Ever Happened to Jim Baldwin? *Omaha World-Herald*, March 25, 1962, p 21

[181] U.S. Headstone Applications for Military Veterans

[182] "Fontenelle Hermit Was Colorful Person," *Evening World-Herald*, June 16, 1966, p 18

About the Author

Marlene is a current board member of the Omaha Walking Club. She enjoys nature and researching local history. She became interested in writing this book after searching for "Omaha Walking Club" in the newspaper archives—just for fun. After clipping over 3,000 newspaper articles, she was hooked. This was a book that needed to be written!

The author on the History Trail at Fontenelle Forest in August 2025